How to Buy Stocks
A Guide to Successful Investing

The floor of the New York Stock Exchange, the nation's biggest market place for securities. Around the edge are the brokers' phone booths, and in the center the trading posts where stocks are bought and sold at public auction.

How to Buy Stocks

A Guide to Successful Investing

by

LOUIS ENGEL

Little, Brown and Company · *Boston*

Published April 1953
Reprinted April 1953 (three times)
Reprinted May 1953 (three times)
Reprinted August 1953
Reprinted December 1953 (twice)
Reprinted March 1954
Reprinted May 1954
Reprinted October 1954

Published simultaneously
in Canada by McClelland and Stewart Limited

PRINTED IN THE UNITED STATES OF AMERICA

TO
C. E. M.
*who formed a new philosophy of investing
to fit a new phase of capitalism*

Foreword

THIS book is based on a very simple premise: that the stock market is going up.

Tomorrow? Next month? Next year?

Maybe yes, maybe no. Maybe the market will be a lot lower then than it is today.

But over any long period of time — ten years, twenty years, fifty years — this book assumes that the market is bound to go up.

Why?

Because it always has.

Because the market is a measure of the vigor of American business, and unless something drastic happens to America, business is going to go on growing.

Because prices of food and clothing and almost everything else in the country — including stocks — have steadily gone up as the buying power of the dollar has dwindled. That's a trend that isn't likely to be reversed.

And so these are the reasons why the author is sold on the idea of investing, of buying stocks for the long pull — not for a quick profit tomorrow.

There's nothing hidden about this prejudice. You'll see it when you read the book. And you will find other prejudices, other opinions, despite an earnest effort to focus this book strictly on facts — the facts about investing that have been obscured all too long by double talk, by financial jargon, and by unnecessary mystery.

Of course, it can be said that there are no facts when you get beyond the simple business of adding one and one. That's true. So let's say that here are the facts as the author sees them — and as plainly as he can state them.

He has only one hope: that they will add up to good common sense in your own mind.

LOUIS ENGEL

January 25, 1953

Acknowledgments

SUCH is the process of learning that it is never possible for anyone to say exactly how he acquired any given body of knowledge. And that circumstance I now find somewhat consoling, because in a very real sense, this book is not my book, but it is the product of hundreds of different people who over the years have taught me what I have simply written down here.

Obviously, I cannot acknowledge my indebtedness to all these people — many of them I do not even know — and so I must necessarily limit my thanks to those who helped me directly in the preparation and checking of the material in this book.

These include Cecil MacCoy, Willard K. Vanderbeck, and F. W. Reiniger of the New York Stock Exchange; Howard T. Sprow of Chadbourne, Hunt, Jaeckel & Brown; John W. Adams, Jr., of Albert-Frank-Guenther Law, Inc.; John McKenzie and George Olsen of Standard & Poor's Corporation; J. A. Livingston of the *Philadelphia Bulletin;* Max Fromkin of Fromkin & Fromkin; J. Scott Rattray of the Toronto Stock Exchange; and a score of individuals actively engaged in the securities business — Kenneth R. Williams, Robert L. Stott, Victor B. Cook, Edward A. Pierce, Milija Rubezanin, James E.

Thomson, Donald T. Regan, Peter F. McCourt, William H. Board, Stanley H. Challenger, Rudolph J. Chval, James D. Corbett, T. Gordon Crotty, John F. Ferguson, Calvin Gogolin, Austin A. Graham, Dave Hyatt, Richard C. Jamieson, Gillette K. Martin, Anthony G. Meyer, Harvey L. Miller, Allen A. Pierce, Walter A. Scholl, Julius H. Sedlmayr, Frank L. Spangler, and — last but certainly not least — Elizabeth J. Gibson and Muriel D. Nutzel.

Contents

How to Buy Stocks

A Guide to Successful Investing

Chapter 1
What It Means to Invest

THIS is a book about how to make your money earn more money for you by investing it.

It is not a book about how to make a million in the stock market. If there were any certain way to do that, all the brokers in the world, the men who are supposed to know more than most people about the market, would be millionaires. They're not. As a matter of fact, precious few of them are.

This is a book about investing. Specifically, it's a book about investing in stocks and bonds, which is one way of putting your extra money to work so that in the long run it will earn a good return for you, in the form of regular income or a profit or both.

Most people, if they have anything left at all after paying their bills, will think first of putting that extra money into the savings bank or into life insurance. Nobody could possibly quarrel with such a prudent course, because those forms of investment are essential if a man is going to protect himself properly against the always unpredictable emergencies of life.

But today millions of people have come to regard *securities* — stocks and bonds in all their varied forms — as another equally good form of investment.

3

Of course, there's a risk in buying stocks and bonds — and for most people it's a far bigger risk than it needs to be because they've never taken the time to study securities or find out how to invest wisely.

But it should never be forgotten that there's some risk in any form of investment. There's a risk in just having money. Actually, it's a double-barreled risk. The one risk — the risk that you might lose some of your money regardless of how you invest it — is always evident. The other risk is never so apparent. And that's the risk that the money you save today may not buy as much at some future time if prices of food and clothing and almost everything else continue to go up, as indeed they have more or less steadily since this country began. The man who simply hoards his extra dollars may avoid that first *evident* risk — the risk of losing any of them — but he can never sidestep the *unseen* risk, the risk of inflation.

So every decision you make about what to do with your extra money should take into consideration those two kinds of risk — the *evident* and the *unseen*.

Naturally, too, you must also consider the return you hope to realize on your money. In most forms of investment the greater the return you try to get, the greater the risk — the *evident* risk — you must be prepared to take.

If you put your money in a savings account, it's almost impossible to lose money, because your savings are insured up to $10,000 by the Federal Deposit Insurance Corporation. But you have to be willing to accept a return of only 1% or 2% or 2½% interest a year, and you have to realize that a savings

4

account provides no protection against the *unseen* risk of inflation. Your money or capital won't grow except by the redeposit of the interest you get and then only slowly.

Life insurance is also virtually 100% safe, thanks to state and federal laws. But there's more sense in buying life insurance to protect your family than there is buying it as an investment. Over a long period of years, a life insurance policy may yield a return somewhat better than that of a savings account, but it too fails to protect you against the *unseen* risk. The money you may get on a life insurance policy when you retire is not likely to buy as much as you could have bought with all the money you paid out on premiums over the years.

What else might you do with your money? Well, you might put it into a savings and loan association which makes a business of lending money on home mortgages. Thanks again to government supervision, that kind of investment on your part will be relatively safe as far as the *evident* risk is concerned but it will probably pay you only a little more interest than you would get on a savings account, and it will not protect you against the *unseen* risk of inflation.

You can invest in real estate. And as a general rule real estate prices are likely to rise if the prices of other things do. So there is protection there, you say, against that *unseen* risk. Yes, there is — *provided* you buy the right piece of property at the right time and at the right figure, and provided you're just as lucky when you sell it. Provided too that all the taxes you pay while you own the property don't eat up your potential profit, and provided you cope with all the unpredictable actions of local zoning and assessment boards. Here the *evident* risks are so great, even for those who work full time at buying, developing, managing, and selling properties, that real estate must be classified not as an investment but as a speculation for the *average* man with only a little extra money.

Finally, you can invest in stocks and bonds. That's what savings banks do with at least part of the money you deposit with them in order to earn the interest they pay you and to earn a profit for themselves. The same thing is true of insurance companies. Both kinds of institutions have always invested heavily in bonds, but today they are buying more and more stocks to the limits permitted by the several state laws. Furthermore, commercial banks and trust companies that are responsible for funds left with them to invest for various beneficiaries are putting a greater proportion of those funds into stocks.

Why?

Because over the years, the record shows that the average stock has paid a better return and provided a better balance of protection against the *evident* and *unseen* risks than any other form of investment.

The *stockholders* of America are the people who own, operate, and finance much of its business — virtually all its more important business. As that business has grown, stock owners have prospered. As it continues to grow, they will continue to prosper.

Not all of them have prospered all the time. Of course not. But most of them have most of the time. Some have made millions, and some have gone broke, just as some companies have succeeded and some have failed. But over the years, the average investor has earned from 3% to 7% on his money. Most important of all, he has seen his stockholdings go up in value as prices generally have risen, and he has thus protected his money against the *unseen* risk of inflation.

These are the reasons why thousands and thousands of people are buying stocks today who never gave them a thought until very recently. And uniformly they're finding that it pays to know something about the fundamentals of the business. So . . .

Chapter 2
What Are Common Stocks?

THERE'S nothing commonplace about *common stock*. It's the Number 1 security in our system, basic to all corporate business. If you own a *share* of *stock* in a company, you own part of that company. You and the other shareholders own the company *in common*.

How does common stock come into being?

Assume for the moment that you've invented a fine, new collapsible metal fishing rod. You've got your patents and you're convinced there is a splendid market for your Pocket Fishing Pole.

You're all ready to begin production, except for that one essential: *capital*. You haven't got the money to rent a small factory, buy the necessary machinery, and hire labor and salesmen. You could get your business under way for $20,-000, but you haven't got $20,000. The bank won't lend it to you simply on the strength of your patents, and you can't find an "angel" with that kind of cash to put in your business.

So you decide to form a company and sell shares in the enterprise. You file the necessary incorporation papers as required by your state law, and the Pocket Pole Company, Incorporated, comes into being.

In setting that company up you might find twenty men, each of whom was willing to put up an even thousand dollars. In that case you'd only have to issue and sell twenty shares of stock at a thousand dollars apiece. Then every man who bought such a share would own 1/20 of the company.

But one man might be willing to put two thousand dollars into your Pocket Pole Company, while another man could only afford to invest two hundred dollars. So instead of issuing 20 shares of stock at $1000 each, you decide it's better to put a lower price on every share of stock and sell more shares. Such a plan would be more attractive to the people who might be interested in buying the stock because if they ever had to sell it, they would probably find it easier to dispose of lower-priced shares. After all, more people can spare $10 or $100 than can afford to invest in $1000 units.

So you finally decide to *issue* 2000 shares at $10 apiece. That's the common stock of the Pocket Pole Co., Inc., and the $10 is the figure you set as its *par value*.

You sell the 2000 shares at $10 apiece, and by this means you raise the $20,000 capital you need. The Pocket Pole Company is in business. Actually, of course, you might well think of Pocket Pole as *your* business, and when the company was set up you might conclude special arrangements with the other stockholders whereby you could acquire a stock interest in the company at little or no cost to yourself, but for purposes of simplicity it can be assumed here that you simply buy your stock like any other stockholder.

Every man who owns a share of Pocket Pole stock is a stockholder in the company. He is a share owner, a part owner.

How big a part of the company he owns depends on how many shares he buys in relation to the 2000 which are sold or outstanding. If he buys 1 share he owns 1/2000 of the company. If he buys 20 shares he owns 1/100, or 1% of the company. As evidence of his ownership, a *stock certificate* is issued to each stockholder showing the number of shares he owns.

When the stock is all sold, the company finds that it has 50 stockholders on its books. Now it would be difficult to operate Pocket Pole if all 50 of them had to be consulted about every major decision — whether to buy this lathe or that one, whether to price the product at $20 or $25.

So the stockholders elect a *board of directors* to oversee the operations of the company. How is the board picked? By the stockholders on the basis of the number of shares of stock each man owns. If there are five men to be elected to the board, each for a set term, the man who owns one share of stock will as a matter of general practice be allowed one vote for each of the five vacancies, and the man who owns ten shares will have ten votes.

This five-man board of directors elects its own chairman, and once organized, it is responsible for managing the affairs of the Pocket Pole Company. Since in most instances the board members can't give their full time to the job of running the company, they pick a president to be the actual operating head, and they also name the other major officers. Such officers may or may not be members of the board, but they are responsible to the full board, and periodically — perhaps once a month or once a quarter — the officers report to the board on the progress of the company and their conduct of its affairs.

Then once a year the Pocket Pole Company board of directors will conduct a meeting open to all the stockholders at which the management makes its *annual report* to the owners. Furthermore, the board supplies all stockholders, those present and those absent, with a copy of the report.

If any stockholder is dissatisfied with the way things are going, he can speak his mind at the meeting. He may even make a motion that the board adopt some policy or procedure that he thinks is a better one, and if the motion is in order, it will be submitted to the stockholders for a vote. In most instances, such issues are decided by a simple majority vote with each stockholder being allowed as many votes as he has shares.

If an action that requires a vote of the share owners is scheduled to come before a meeting, such as the election of new directors, each stockholder is notified, and if he cannot attend the *annual meeting* and vote, he is usually asked to let one or more of the officers or directors act as his *proxy* or representative and vote for him. Sometimes when new directors are to be elected, a dissident group of stockholders will propose a rival slate in opposition to those picked by the management. In such a fight, each camp is likely to solicit proxies from the stockholders.

In addition to the regular meetings of the board or the annual meeting of the stockholders, special meetings of either group may be called to deal with special problems.

Why should anybody invest his money in the Pocket Pole

Company? Because he thinks it has a good product and one that is likely to make money. If it does, he as a part owner stands to make money. That can happen in two ways: First, through the payment of dividends and secondly through an increase in the value of Pocket Pole stock.

Let's look at the dividend picture first. Suppose in the first year the company makes a net profit after paying all its bills and taxes of $2000 or 10% on its $20,000 *capitalization,* the money it raised by selling 2000 shares of common stock. That would be a handsome profit for a new company but not impossible.

It would then be up to the board of directors to decide what to do with that profit. It could pay it all out to the stockholders in *dividends,* or it could vote to keep every penny of it in the company treasury and use it to buy more machinery to make more Pocket Poles and earn more profit the following year. Since all stockholders like dividends and all boards of directors know that, Pocket Pole's board might very properly decide on a middle course. It might vote to pay out $1000 in dividends and plow the other $1000 back into the business.

Now if the board has $1000 for dividends and 2000 shares of stock outstanding, the dividend per share is going to be 50¢. That's what the man with 1 share of stock gets, while the man with 10 shares gets $5, and the man with 100 shares $50. For all of them that would represent a 5% return on their investment, regardless of the number of shares they own.

But there's also another intangible return that they get on their money. Presumably that $1000 which the board decided to retain and plow back into business will serve to increase the value of every man's share in the company — his *equity* in the company, as it's called in financial lingo.

If an original share of stock in Pocket Pole was fairly valued at $10, each of the 2000 shares might now be considered worth $10.50, since the company has an extra thousand dollars in addition to the original capital of $20,000.

Already that par value figure of $10 has been made slightly fictitious, and as the years roll by it will bear no real relation to the value of the stock, if the company continues to earn good money and if the directors continue, year after year, to put a portion of those earnings back into the company. In comparatively few years, the total *assets* of the company — everything it owns, its plant, machinery, and products — might well be doubled without any increase in its *liabilities* — what the company owes. In that case, the *book value* of each share of stock — tangible assets, less liabilities, divided by the number of shares outstanding — would also be doubled.

Par value is a term so generally misunderstood and so completely without significance that many companies today either do not set any value on their stock, in which case it is known as *no par stock*, or they fix the value at $1 or $5, a figure so low that it could not possibly be considered an index of its real value.

Even book value is a term with little real meaning today, although it had a real significance in the last century when *watered stock* was all too often sold to an unsuspecting public. That graphic phrase, watered stock, is supposed to have had its origin in the practice of feeding cattle large quantities of salt on their way to market and then giving them a big drink of water just before they went on the weighing scales.

As applied to securities, the phrase describes that kind of common stock which was issued with an inflated value. For instance, an unscrupulous operator might pay only half a million dollars for some company, then issue one million dollars' worth of stock in it. He might sell all that stock to others and pocket a half million profit, or after he sold half the stock and got his cost back, he might keep the remaining shares and thus own a half interest in the company at no cost to himself. Such stock issues are now virtually nonexistent, thanks to improved business ethics and government regulation.

Most stockholders have come to realize that book value doesn't mean very much. What counts is the earning power of a company, not the total value of its plants and machinery. The stock of many a big company sells frequently at a price considerably more than its book value — sometimes double or triple the book value. In contrast, other stocks, like those of the railroads which have gigantic investments in equipment, sell for much less than book value. Book value is frequently thought of as representing what the owner of a share of stock could expect to get if the company were *liquidated* — if it went out of business and sold off all its property. This is often a misconception, because when a company is in liquidation, it can rarely get full value for the property it must dispose of.

So how do you know what a share of stock is worth — Pocket Pole stock or any other?

There's only one answer to that. Bluntly, it's only worth

what somebody else is willing to pay for it when you want to sell it.

If the product isn't popular and sales suffer, if the cost of wages and raw materials is too high, if the management is inefficient, Pocket Pole or any other company can fail. And if it goes into bankruptcy, your stock can be valueless.

That's the black side of the picture. That's what can happen if the risk proves to be a bad one.

But if Pocket Pole proves to be a successful company, if it has a consistent record of good earnings, if part of those earnings are paid out regularly in dividends and another part of them wisely used to expand the company — then your stock is likely to be worth more than the $10 you paid for it. Perhaps a good deal more.

And that is the second way in which the stockholder expects to make money on his investment. First, through dividends. Second, through an increase in the value of his stock — or rather an increase in the price of it, which may be something entirely different.

The price of a stock, like the price of almost everything else in this world, is determined by supply and demand — what one man is willing to pay for a stock and what another one is willing to sell it for, what one man *bids* and another man *asks*.

Here, in brief, is the story of common stock — what it is, how it comes into being, what it means to own it.

General Motors, General Electric, American Telephone & Telegraph may have millions of shares of stock outstanding and they may count their shareholders in the hundreds of thousands, but in these giant corporations, each share of stock pays precisely the same kind of role as a share of stock in our Pocket Pole Company, and each stockholder has the same rights, privileges, and responsibilities.

There is only one significant difference between buying a share of Pocket Pole and investing in a share of General Motors, General Electric, or American Telephone & Telegraph. These big companies have been in business for many years. You know something about them and the reputations they enjoy. You know how good their products are. You can examine their financial history, see for yourself how the prices of their stocks have moved over the years and what kind of record they have made as far as earnings and dividends are concerned. And on the basis of such information you can form a more reliable judgment about whether the stocks of these companies are overpriced or underpriced.

In contrast, the man who buys stock in our Pocket Pole Company has nothing to go on other than his own estimate of how good a product the company has and how big its sales are likely to be. There are no bench marks to guide him, no past records on which to base an appraisal of the future.

As a matter of literal truth, the Pocket Pole stockholder cannot properly be called an investor. Most times when a man buys stock in a brand-new company he isn't investing in it; he's speculating in it. An *investor* is a man who is willing to take a moderate risk with his money for the sake of earning a moderate return, which in the case of common stocks might mean annual dividends averaging about 5% or 6%. A *speculator* is a man who takes a big risk for the sake of making a big profit because of an increase in the price of a stock. An investor usually has his eye on long-term values to be realized over a period of years; a speculator hopes to make a profit in a relatively short period of time.

American business needs both kinds of risk takers. Without the speculator, new businesses wouldn't be born nor many an old business tided over a rough spot. Without the investor, a company would not have the capital to carry on, much less grow and expand.

Chapter 3
How and Why New Stock Is Issued

LET'S assume that the years are good to our Pocket Pole Co., Inc. It continues to grow. The original collapsible fishing pole has proved a best seller, and the company now has a full line of models. Good earnings year after year have enabled the management to put the stock on a regular annual dividend basis. It now pays $1 a year per share — 25¢ a quarter — and in several good years the directors even declared *extra dividends,* one of 25¢ and two of 50¢ a share.

Now the company feels that the time has come when it should expand. It could sell twice as many Pocket Poles, make twice as much profit, if it only had a bigger factory. So the board of directors decides to expand the plant. That means it will need more machinery, more manpower, and above all things, more money — a lot more money than it has in the company treasury. Problem: How to get about $40,000.

A bank might advance the money. Maybe two or three banks would each put up part of the loan. But some of the directors don't like the idea of being in hock to the banks. They worry not only about paying 4% or 5% interest on the loan every year but also about paying the money back in instalments. That kind of steady drain on the company treasury for years ahead could eat into earnings and result in few if any dividends. Furthermore, to protect their loans, the banks might insist on having their representatives sit on the board of directors — and that is a prospect some of the directors don't relish.

Isn't there some other way to raise the money?

Maybe the present stockholders would like to put more money into the company. Maybe there are other people who would like to invest in a nice thriving little business like Pocket Pole. There's an idea.

And so the board of directors proposes to the stockholders that they authorize the company to issue 3000 additional shares of stock — 2000 shares to be sold at once, and the remaining 1000 to be held against the day when the company may want to raise more money by selling more stock. Each of the new shares of stock will carry with it the same rights and privileges as an original share.

This proposal is approved by a substantial majority of the stockholders, but not without some disagreement. One stockholder objected to the plan. He thought the company should have two classes of common stock — a Class A stock which would consist of the original issue, enjoying full rights and privileges, and a new Class B stock on which the same dividends would be paid but which would not carry any voting privileges. In other words, he wanted control of the company kept in the hands of the original stockholders.

The board chairman replied to this suggestion by pointing out that such *classified-stock* setups, A stock and B stock, are no longer popular with investors. True, some companies like Columbia Broadcasting and R. J. Reynolds Tobacco still have two issues of common stock outstanding, and so do many Canadian companies, but few United States firms have followed such a practice on new stock issues in recent years.

Furthermore, the chairman explained that the old stockholders would probably still retain about the same measure of control since they would probably buy most of the new stock issue anyway. This appeared likely because it would be offered to them first and on especially favorable terms. This is usual procedure for companies that have new stock to sell.

In this instance, the board recommended that old stockholders be permitted to buy the new stock at $20 a share, or just $2 below what the old stock was then worth, while others who might buy any of the issue that was left over would have to pay the going price at the time.

After the stockholders approved the plan, each of them was offered the *right* to subscribe to the new stock in proportion to his present holdings, and this right was clearly set forth in a warrant or certificate. Every man who owned one of the original 2000 shares was permitted to buy one of the new 2000 shares at $20. And the man with 10 old shares could buy 10 new ones. The rights had to be exercised within two weeks, for most rights are relatively short-lived, although some are occasionally issued that are good for a period of years, and in the financial community these are not usually called rights but *warrants*.

Some Pocket Pole shareholders, unable or unwilling to purchase additional stock, sold their rights. Often the market in such rights is a brisk one, even when they entitle the holder to buy only a part of a share — a tenth, a fifth, or a quarter of a share of new stock for each old share that he owns.

In the case of Pocket Pole each right was worth $1. Here is the way that value would be arrived at. If you owned one share of Pocket Pole worth $22 and you exercised your right to buy an additional share at $20, you would then own two shares at an average of $21 apiece, or just $1 less than the going price per share. Hence the right could be figured to have a value of just $1. Actually, some stockholders might sell their rights for a fraction of that, while others might get more than $1 apiece, if the price of Pocket Pole advanced while the rights were still on the market. And of course, some careless stockholders would ignore their rights, forgetting either to sell or exercise them.

When the rights expired, Pocket Pole discovered that all of them had been exercised except for 50 shares of the new issue, and these were readily sold at a price of $22. The company had raised $40,100 of new capital, and now had 4000 shares of common stock outstanding.

Pocket Pole's plan for expanding the plant was put into effect, but because of delays in getting the machinery it needed, it was two years until the new factory was in full operation. That situation raised for the board the awkward problem of how to continue paying dividends to the stockholders. In the first year of the transition period, the board felt obligated to continue paying the customary $1 dividend; but that put a serious dent in the company treasury. The second year the directors decided it would be foolhardy to do that again. They concluded that the only prudent thing they could do was to keep the full year's earnings in the treasury until the new plant was operating efficiently.

But if the company paid no dividend, what would the stockholders say? Omission of the dividend would certainly mean that the price of the stock would go down, for it would be interpreted as a sign of serious trouble by those who might be interested in buying the stock.

The board found an answer to that problem in the 1000 shares of new stock which had been authorized but not issued. With the approval of the stockholders, it took those 1000 shares and distributed them among the owners of the 4000 outstanding shares on the basis of ¼ of a share of free stock for every single share which a stockholder owned.

Actually, this *stock dividend* did nothing to improve the lot of any individual stockholder. He was not one penny richer, nor did he actually own any greater proportion of the company. The man who had 1 share before the stock dividend owned 1/4000 of the company. Now with 1¼ shares out of the 5000 outstanding, he still owned exactly 1/4000.

And yet in terms of future prospects that extra quarter of a share had real potential value. When the company got rolling again, that extra quarter share could represent a real profit and extra dividends, too.

That, happily, is exactly what happened. Pocket Pole prospered. The next year it earned $2 a share, and the directors felt they could prudently restore the old $1 dividend on each share, and to the man who held 1¼ shares that meant a return of $1.25.

Chapter 4

What Are Preferred Stocks?

WITH its new plant and its new machinery, the Pocket Pole Company forged rapidly ahead. Earnings doubled. Then they doubled again. And most of those earnings, by decision of the directors, were reinvested in the business to expand production and improve operations. Dividends were modest. But the company was growing. Now its assets totaled almost $150,000.

Then another problem — and another opportunity — presented itself. The Rapid Reel Company, a well-known competitor owned and operated by a single family, could be acquired for $75,000. It was, the Pocket Pole directors agreed, a good buy at that price, but where could they get the $75,000?

Negotiations with the president of Rapid Reel indicated that he was anxious to retire from business, that he planned to invest whatever he got from the sale of the company so that it would yield him and his family a safe, reasonable income. Further, it was evident that he had a high regard for the management of Pocket Pole and was favorably impressed with the company's prospects. Here was the basis of a deal.

So the directors of Pocket Pole proposed that they take over Rapid Reel as a going concern and merge it into their own. How would they pay for it? By issuing *preferred* stock in the Pocket Pole Company — an issue of 750 shares with a par value of $100 per share — and giving it to the owners of Rapid Reel in exchange for their company.

Like most preferred stock, this issue would guarantee to the owners a prior claim on all assets of Pocket Pole, should it ever be necessary to dissolve the company, and the stock would carry a specific dividend payable every year on every share before any dividends could be paid to common-stock holders. To make the deal as attractive as possible for the owners of Rapid Reel, the company was willing to pay a fairly high dividend — $5 on every share, or 5%.

Ordinarily, such a preferred dividend would not be paid in any given year unless the company earned enough to cover it, but in this case it was provided that the stock was to be an issue of *cumulative preferred*. This meant that if Pocket Pole could not pay the $5 dividend in any year, the amount due for that year would accrue to the preferred-stock holders and would be paid the following year or whenever the company had sufficient earnings to pay it. If the company could not make the payments on the preferred for a period of years, they would continue to accrue during all that time and would have to be paid in full before the common-stock holders got so much as a dime in dividends.

On the other hand, it was agreed that this would not be an issue of *participating preferred*. This meant that the holders of the preferred would not participate, beyond the stipulated dividend payment, in any of the extra profits the company might earn in good years. No matter if earnings were so good that dividends on the common stock were doubled or tripled, the holders of the preferred would still get just their $5 a share and no more. Furthermore, they would have no participation in company affairs and no voting rights excepting on matters that might adversely affect the rights guaranteed them as preferred-stock holders. They were also guaranteed the right to elect two directors to the board if the company should ever pass or fail to pay the preferred dividend for eight consecutive quarters.

Although the terms of this issue might be regarded as fairly typical, there is no such thing as a standard preferred stock. About the only common denominator of all such issues is the guarantee that the owner will be accorded a preferential treatment, ahead of the common-stock holder, in the payment of dividends and in the distribution of any assets that might remain if the company were to be liquidated. That's why it is called preferred stock, and that's why its price usually doesn't fluctuate, either up or down, as much as the price of the company's common stock.

From that point on, specifications vary widely. Most preferreds have a $100 par value, but some are no-par stocks. Dividends range from 3% up to 6% or 7% and even more on some preferreds that were sold years ago when interest rates on money were higher than they are today. Most preferreds are nonparticipating, but there are many exceptions.

Many preferreds are issued, as Pocket Pole proposed, to acquire another company, but most of them are issued simply to acquire more capital for expansion or improvements at a time when the company's circumstances are such that its stockholders and the public at large might not be willing to invest in more of its common stock.

Cumulative preferreds are by all odds the most common, but there are some noncumulative issues on the market — principally those of railroads. Occasionally, on cumulative preferreds, accrued dividends pile up in bad years to a point where it becomes impossible for a company to pay them. In such a situation, it may attempt to negotiate a settlement with the preferred holders on the basis of a partial payment. However, some companies have paid off more than $100 a share in accumulated back dividends on their $100 preferreds.

Another kind of preferred stock that has become increasingly popular in recent years is the *convertible preferred*. Such a stock carries a provision permitting the owner to convert it into a specified number of shares of common stock. Suppose, for instance, that a company were to sell a new issue of convertible preferred at a time when its common stock was quoted at $17 or $18 a share; in such a situation, the conversion clause might provide that every share of the new $100 preferred could be exchanged for five shares of the company's common stock at any time in the next five years. Obviously, there would be no advantage to the preferred-stock holder in making such a swap unless the common stock advanced in price to more than $20 a share.

The price of a convertible is apt to fluctuate more than the price of other preferreds because a convertible is always tied to the common stock of a company. This has its good and bad points. If the company is successful and the price of its common stock rises, the holder of a convertible preferred will find that his stock has had a corresponding increase in value, since it can be exchanged for the common. On the other hand, if the common declines, the convertible preferred is apt to suffer too, because one of the features which was counted on to make it attractive has suddenly lost something of its value, and the other features of the issue, such as its dividend rate, may not prove as attractive or substantial as those of orthodox preferreds. Convertibles are always especially popular when stock prices are rising generally.

Most preferreds carry a provision which permits the company to *call* in the issue and pay it off at full value, plus a premium of perhaps 5%. A company will usually exercise this right to call its preferred stock if it thinks it can replace the outstanding issue with one that carries a lower dividend rate.

From the point of view of the owners of Rapid Reel, the plan which Pocket Pole proposed looked attractive. So they accepted it — after the common-stock holders of Pocket Pole had approved the plan and authorized issuance of 750 shares of 5% cumulative-preferred stock in exchange for the Rapid Reel Company.

With this acquisition, Pocket Pole was on its way to becoming big business. And in the next ten years, with booming sales, it strode forward along that path with seven-league boots.

It bought the little Nylon Line Company for cash.

It acquired the Fishing Supplies Corporation by another issue of preferred stock which it called second-preferred, because it had to recognize the prior claim to assets and earnings that had been granted the owners of Rapid Reel. To make

27

this issue more attractive to the owners of Fishing Supplies, a conversion privilege was included in it.

It bought the Sure-Fire Rifle Company by selling an additional issue of common stock and arranging to trade the Sure-Fire stockowners one share of Pocket Pole for every three shares of Sure-Fire that they owned.

Finally, it acquired control of Camping Supplies, Incorporated, on a similar stock-swapping basis.

Now, with a full, well-rounded line of all kinds of fishing, hunting, and camping supplies, backed by an aggressive advertising and merchandising campaign, the company experimented with its own retail outlets. In a few years, these grew into a small chain of 30 sporting-goods stores, known as the Rod & Reel Centers.

Sales multiplied, and so did earnings — up to $10 and $12 a share. Dividends were boosted correspondingly, and with the adoption of a regular $6 annual dividend, Pocket Pole stock was frequently quoted at $120 a share and higher. Stockholders complained that it was too high-priced, that it couldn't be sold easily if they wanted to dispose of their holdings.

So the company decided to *split* the stock on a 10-for-1 basis and simultaneously to change its corporate name to Rod & Reel, Incorporated — a much more appropriate name, since most fishermen consider the fishing "pole" passé. Hence it issued new certificates for ten shares of Rod & Reel common stock for every single share of the old Pocket Pole stock. Theoretically, each of the new shares should have been worth about $12, but such is the nature of *stock splits* that before long, without any significant change in the outlook for the company, the new shares were being bought and sold at around $15.

This is the story of Rod & Reel, Inc., formerly Pocket Pole Co., Inc. It is a success story, as it was meant to be to show the various kinds of stock operations that may mark a company's growth. But for that matter, it is no more of a success story than the real-life stories of General Motors or Coca-Cola or International Business Machines or any of hundreds of other companies in which the original investors (or speculators) saw the value of their stockholdings multiplied 10, 20, even 100 times over.

Chapter 5
Bonds — and the Investment Banker

DO you have a lot of money to invest — say $40,000 or $50,000?

If you do, then you ought to know about *corporate bonds,* the kind of bonds that are issued by companies like Rod & Reel, Inc., and bought principally by *institutional investors* — banks, insurance companies, and charitable foundations.

If you don't have that much money, you can skip this chapter, if you wish, because chances are that there are better investments for you than corporate bonds.

But who can tell when you may get a lot of money? And anyway, every intelligent investor should know something about bonds just to fill in a vital part of the background.

The easiest way to understand them is to consider the plight of Rod & Reel's treasurer at a time when the company needed half a million dollars of new capital — a much greater sum than any it had ever had to raise before.

It needed that money because over the years it had grown pretty haphazardly, acquiring a manufacturing plant here and another one there, a warehouse here and some retail stores there.

Now the whole operation had to be pulled together, made to function efficiently. An independent firm of engineers had figured just what economies Rod & Reel could effect by centralizing most of its manufacturing operations in one big new plant and modernizing its equipment. In the long run, the half-million dollars would unquestionably prove to be money well spent.

But how to get the money?

As company treasurer, you might first discuss the matter with the officers of your regular bank. They are perfectly willing to supply you from month to month with the credit you need for raw materials, but a half-million-dollar loan to build a new plant — well, that is not for them. What you need in the present situation, they suggest, is help from a very special kind of banker, an investment banker.

Investment bankers specialize in raising the kind of money that business needs for long-term use, usually in amounts considerably greater than the half-million Rod & Reel wanted.

Most times when a company wants money, it prefers to get it without any strings attached — without obligating itself to pay any set return. In short, it wants *venture capital, equity capital,* the kind of money it can only get by selling common stock.

If the company's condition is sound, if its prospects are good, and if the stock market is then very active and healthy, an investment banker may agree to *underwrite* such an issue. That means he will buy all of the new stock himself from the company, and then resell it at a set price per share to individual buyers. As a general rule, this is the only time in the entire life of a stock issue that its price will be fixed — at the time when it is originally issued, either to start a new company or raise new capital. Once the stock is in public hands, its price will be determined solely by how much the buyer will pay and how much the seller wants for the stock he owns.

For the risk that the investment banker assumes, the risk that he may not be able to resell the entire issue that he has bought, he expects to make a profit on each share of the issue.

On small issues, involving only one or two million dollars, he may be able and willing to carry the whole risk himself, but on most issues he shares the risk with other investment bankers who join with him in forming an *underwriting group* under his management.

When it comes time to sell the issue to the public, the underwriters usually invite other security dealers to join with them in a *selling group* or *syndicate*.

The costs of underwriting and selling an issue of stock depend primarily on how salable the underwriting group thinks the issue will be when it is put on the market. Those costs might run anywhere from 3% to 10% of the final selling price. On some issues, such as cheap mining or oil stocks offered at a dollar or two a share, charges might even run as high as 20%, for these *penny stocks* can usually be sold only by costly merchandising effort. Half of the total commission on any new issue might go to those who underwrite it and half to those who sell it, but if the issue looks as though it might be "sticky" or hard to sell, the selling commission is likely to be increased and the underwriting commission reduced correspondingly.

Whenever a company wants to raise capital by selling a new securities issue it may well shop around to see which investment banker will offer the best terms and handle the new issue at the lowest commission cost. Once a bid is accepted, the relationship between the company and the underwriter is apt to develop naturally into a close one, and if the company needs to raise additional capital at some future time, it may well expect to get help again from the same underwriter, and it may not even ask for other bids.

By law or government regulation, however, public utilities are generally required to submit any new securities issue to *competitive bidding*. Competitive bids are also compulsory on railroad securities, but the Interstate Commerce Commission, which exercises control in this field, usually exempts the railroads from this requirement.

While most companies might prefer to raise new capital by selling stock, this is not the kind of securities issue which an investment banker is most likely to sanction in the case of a small company like Rod & Reel. He is more apt to suggest an issue of bonds rather than an issue of stock. In normal years, the aggregate value of new bond issues exceeds the value of new stock issues by 3- or 4-to-1.

Bonds always represent borrowed money which the company that issues them is obligated to repay. That's why they are called obligations. They are a kind of promissory note. When a company sells bonds, it borrows the money from the buyers, and the bonds stand as a formal evidence of that debt. Each bond is an agreement on the part of the company to repay the face value of the bond—usually $1000—at a specified time and to pay a set annual rate of *interest* from the day it is issued to the day it is redeemed.

The man who buys stock in a company actually buys a part of that company. The man who buys a company's bonds simply lends his money to the company. The stockholder expects to collect dividends on his stock and thus share in the company's profits. The bondholder expects to earn a fixed return on his investment in the form of interest payments.

There's one other important difference between stocks and bonds. If a company is successful, the stockholder can hope to make a substantial profit because the price of his stock should go up. The bondholder enjoys no such extravagant hope. No matter how successful a company is, the price of its bonds rarely advances more than a small percentage.

On the other hand, if the bondholder can't expect to gain as much on his capital, neither does he stand to lose as much. His investment is much better protected, thanks to the fact that bonds do represent debt, and if a company is dissolved, the debt it owes its bondholders, like any other debt it owes for labor and materials, must be paid before the stockholders, either common or preferred, can get a nickel out of what's left of the company. The claims of bondholders come first, then the preferred-stock holders — and last, the common-stock holders.

It is because the element of risk in bonds is comparatively so slight that they are such a popular form of investment with banks and insurance companies as well as wealthy people. This is the market the investment banker has his eye on when he underwrites a bond issue, and because it is such a good market, the underwriting and selling commissions are usually much lower on an issue of bonds than on an issue of stock. Other-

34

wise, the two kinds of securities are issued and sold in much the same way.

From the point of view of any company treasurer, bonds have obvious disadvantages as compared with stock. The interest that must be paid on them represents a fixed charge that has to be met in bad times as well as good times, and the bonds must be paid off when they come due. The common-stock holder has to be paid only if the company makes money — and even that is not a binding obligation.

On the other hand, if the company is successful, it doesn't mind having to pay 3% or 4% interest on the money borrowed from bondholders if it can make 10% or 15% profit on that extra capital. Again, bond interest payments are an expense item deducted from a company's earnings before it pays its federal income *tax* on those earnings. In contrast, dividends are paid out of what is left after a company has paid the tax on its earnings. Thus, it actually costs a company less to pay a given amount of money to bondholders than it does to pay the same amount of money to stockholders, because it gets a tax deduction on the one and not on the other.

From the investor's point of view, the best bonds are those that have behind them the strongest assurance that they will be repaid — in full and with the specified interest.

Here the situation is not much different from what it would be if you as an individual sought to get a loan from a bank. If the banker knew you and knew you would be able to repay the money, he might lend it to you without asking you to put up any collateral, such as your life insurance policies or other property, to guarantee the loan. But if it were a sizable loan, he might even insist that you give him a mortgage on your home.

It's much the same way with companies when they issue bonds. They would prefer to get the money without posting their property as a guarantee that the contract set in the bond will be fulfilled. That, as a matter of fact, is precisely the way the Rod & Reel treasurer felt when the investment banker said that the company would have to float a bond issue, not a stock issue.

As long as it had to be bonds, the treasurer proposed that his company issue a half-million dollars of debentures.

A *debenture* is a bond that is backed only by the general credit of the corporation. No specific real estate or property stands as security behind it. It is, in effect, a giant-size I.O.U. Debentures are the most common type of bond issued by big, well-established industrial companies today, and they are being favored increasingly by public utilities. But in the case of Rod & Reel, the investment banker was not disposed to feel that such an issue would be in order, because the company, though successful, was still relatively small and not too well known. He was afraid the debentures wouldn't sell.

The treasurer then asked if a debenture might not be made more attractive by including a convertible provision in it. There are many *convertible bonds* on the market and their terms vary widely, but like convertible preferreds, all of them offer the owner the privilege of converting his bond into a specified number of shares of common stock.

Such a provision may add a certain speculative appeal to the bond — the chance to make an extra profit if the common stock rises — but the typical bond buyer may look askance at such a "sweetener." He knows better than most security buyers that you don't get something for nothing in a security, any more than you do in any other kind of merchandise. A convertible bond may offer the possibility of price appreciation, but its guarantee of safety may not be quite as substantial.

In Rod & Reel's case, the investment banker did not feel that a convertible was feasible, and in the light of his attitude, the treasurer did not even raise the question of whether the company could issue some kind of *income* or *adjustment bond*.

These bonds are a kind of hybrid security, something like a noncumulative preferred stock, since they provide that the interest is to be paid on the bond only as it is earned. If earnings are sufficient to pay only a part of the interest on such bonds, the company must make whatever payment it can to the nearest one half of 1%; thus on a 5% bond a company might pay only 2½% or 3 or 3½%, depending on its earnings.

There is still another kind of bond, the *collateral-trust bond*, which like the income bond used to be more popular than it is today, but Rod & Reel's circumstances were such that this type of security was obviously not suited to them. When a company issues a collateral-trust bond, it deposits securities with a trustee — not its own securities — as a guarantee that the bonds will be redeemed and interest paid on them. Usually the securities on deposit are worth at least 25% more than the total value of the bond issue, and they are frequently the securities of subsidiary companies.

As the discussions progressed, it became apparent that the investment banker felt there was only one kind of bond that

Rod and Reel could offer, and that was a *first-mortgage bond* — the kind of bond which is secured by a mortgage on all of a company's property, not only its existing property but sometimes even on all property which it might later acquire.

These bonds are considered to be among the highest-grade security investments, because they offer the investor an undisputed first claim on company earnings and the greatest possible safety. That first mortgage takes absolute precedence over the claims of all other owners of a company's securities, including the holders of debentures, adjustment bonds, or secondary-mortgage bonds that may be issued after a first mortgage has been made.

Having resigned himself to the fact that Rod & Reel would have to mortgage its property, including the new plant which it expected to build, in order to float a half-million-dollar bond issue, the treasurer next took up with the banker the question of what rate of interest the company might have to pay. Here the banker was in no position to hazard even a guess, because the rate a company has to pay always depends on its credit standing and its earning capacity. And these were the crucial factors on which the banker could not commit himself without a thorough, painstaking investigation of all aspects of the company — the kind of survey which every investment banker must make, with the help of outside accountants, engineers, and other specialists, before underwriting any new issue of stocks or bonds.

Bond interest rates vary not only with the health of the company but also with general business conditions. Thus in 1920, AAA bonds — the highest grade there is — paid over

6%, while in 1945, the same grade bonds returned only 2½%. Characteristically today, bond interest rates range around 3% or 3½%, though some lower grade issues pay up to 4% or 4½%.

The interest rate of a bond is frequently referred to as the *coupon* rate, because bonds usually have appended to them a number of detachable coupons, one for each six months of the bond's life. The owner clips each coupon as it comes due and presents it to the company's paying agent for payment. Coupons are used because bonds formerly were not registered on the company's books in the owner's name, as stock certificates are. Instead, they were the property of the bearer — whoever had them at a given time — and hence were called *bearer bonds*. Today, this practice is not always followed. Some bonds are now registered in the owner's name, just like stocks. On some registered bonds, coupons are still used for the payment of interest, but on others the bondholder gets a check automatically from the company.

Just as crucial as the interest rate to any company issuing bonds is the question of *maturity* — how long a life the bonds will have, how soon the company will have to redeem them or pay them off. In general, the stronger the company, the longer the maturities. For a company like Rod & Reel, 10 years might be considered the maximum time limit. Furthermore, the company would probably be required to establish a *sinking fund* and pay enough into it every year to demonstrate that it would ultimately be able to meet its obligations. In view of its building and reorganization plans, Rod & Reel would probably be allowed a one year breathing spell before

39

it had to start putting money into the sinking fund. Some bonds, known as *serial bonds,* are actually paid off in year-by-year installments. Like preferreds, bonds have call provisions which permit a company to redeem them before maturity.

There is a wide variation in how long bond issues run, but a period of 20 or 30 years is about as common as any. Curiously, the railroads have issued bonds with the longest life, and they also have some with about as short a life as any. Many old rail bonds run for 100 years, and some have no maturity date; they were issued in perpetuity—a frank recognition of the fact that no one expects the rails ever to pay all their debt.

At the other end of the scale, with maturities of only 10 or 15 years, are the *equipment trust* obligations. These bonds are the cheapest method by which railroads can acquire new cars and locomotives; some have carried interest rates under $1\frac{1}{2}\%$. On this kind of bond, the equipment itself stands as the guarantee of repayment.

The maturity of a bond can affect the return you realize on it. You can buy a bond with a 4% coupon rate, but it may *yield* you something less—or something more—than 4%, depending on how much you pay for the bond and what its maturity is. If you pay exactly $1000 for a bond and get $40 interest on it every year, you do realize a 4% yield. But if you pay $1050 for the bond, the $40 interest payment obviously represents less than a 4% return on the money you've invested. Furthermore, if you hold the bond until it matures, you will get only $1000 for it on redemption, a loss of $50. If the bond has a 20-year maturity, that $50 loss would represent, in effect, a reduction of $2.50 a year in your interest payment. Furthermore, over the full 20 years you would have lost the amount of interest that you might have earned on that $50.

The net of it all is that if you pay $1050 for a 4% 20-year bond, it will really only yield you about 3.65%. Of course, if you buy the bond at a discount instead of a premium — for $950 instead of $1050 — you will earn more than 4% on it.

When a company like Rod & Reel has a stock or bond issue to raise new capital, such an issue represents new *financing*. But very often preferred stocks or bonds are issued as part of a *refinancing* operation. Thus, when a company refinances, it may seek to substitute some new bond issue for an outstanding one that it issued many years ago — a process known as *refunding*.

Why should such substitution be made? Because it can be to a company's advantage. As business and investment conditions change, it is frequently worth while to call an outstanding issue of bonds or preferred stock on which the company may be paying a high rate of interest. Such an issue can be paid off out of funds raised by the sale of a new issue carrying a lower rate.

Chapter 6
How New Issues Are Regulated

WHENEVER a company like Rod & Reel wants to raise capital by floating a new issue of stocks or bonds, it must comply with the federal law that governs the sale of any such issue offered to the public.

In the boom days of the twenties many a new stock was sold with few facts and lots of glittering promises. In 1933, Congress changed all that. It enacted a new law, widely known as the *Truth in Securities Act,* and then later it set up the Securities & Exchange Commission to administer that law.

The S.E.C. requires *full disclosure* of all the pertinent facts about any company before it makes a *public offering* of new stocks or bonds. The company must file a lengthy *registration statement* with the S.E.C. in which it sets forth the data for the past several years about its financial condition — its assets and its liabilities, what it owns and what it owes. It must also furnish the profit and loss record for this same period. It must describe all of its outstanding securities and their terms and list all its officers and directors, together with their salaries, bonuses, and stock interests in the company. And it must provide a full description of its operations.

If the data appear to be complete and honest, the S.E.C. gives a green light to the new issue. But this does not mean that it passes any judgment whatsoever on the quality of the securities, how good or bad they may be for any investor. A company might want to raise money by the sale of securities to mine uranium in Times Square, but as long as the full facts about the venture were given — if the company stated frankly that it proposed to go ahead simply because some geologist said he *thought* there *might* be uranium down there — the S.E.C. would have to let the issue go on sale.

The S.E.C. also sees that the information which is filed with it is made available to any possible buyer of the new issue. A company is required to put all the essential facts into a printed *prospectus* — usually about 30 or 40 pages long, sometimes even more — and for a full year after the new stock is issued, every security dealer who has the new stock or bond for sale must give a copy of that prospectus not only to everyone who buys the new issue but to everyone from whom he even solicits an order.

Furthermore, during that year, the new issue cannot be advertised except by a *"tombstone"* announcement, in which no information can be provided beyond the name of the issue, its price, its size, and the names of the underwriters and dealers who have it for sale. And above even this austere announcement the underwriters usually insert a precautionary note to the effect that the advertisement is not to be interpreted as an offer to buy or sell the security, since the offer is made only through the prospectus.

But the company's troubles don't even end here. Most of the states also have laws governing the registration and sale of new securities. While the requirements of these so-called *"blue sky" laws* are much like those of the S.E.C., they are sufficiently varied to cause a company a lot of trouble and a good deal of extra expense in filing the necessary forms.

All told, preparing a new issue for sale can be a very expensive undertaking. The bill for preparing the necessary forms and printing a prospectus may run to $15,000 or $20,000, and it can run as high as $100,000. This might be the case if a large company brought out a new stock issue and had to offer rights to all its stockholders, for each of them would have to be supplied with a prospectus. Fees for lawyers and accountants can add a lot more to this bill.

However, the federal law, as well as most state laws, provides an "out" for little companies like Rod & Reel. For instance, if the new issue has a value of not more than $300,000, the company need only file a short registration form with the S.E.C., and it does not have to prepare and distribute a printed prospectus. And if the new issue can be classified as a *private placement* — usually one that will be offered to fewer than 25 buyers — rather than as a public offering, it doesn't even have to be registered with the S.E.C.

In a case like Rod & Reel's, the investment banker would try to qualify the new issue as a private placement by lining up one or two institutional buyers, perhaps an insurance company or a charitable foundation, before the deal was finally set, and that's why he would insist that the issue be of top-flight quality, which in Rod & Reel's case would mean a first mortgage bond.

While the S.E.C. "full disclosure" rules have undoubtedly done much to protect the investor, it is probably also true that they are more exacting than they have to be and that they deter many a company from trying to raise new money for expansion.

Furthermore, it can be argued that the individual investor doesn't really benefit as he should from the protection that is provided him. Most individuals who buy a new issue — and their number is few compared to those who buy securities already on the market — rarely examine the prospectus or understand it if they do. As a matter of fact, if the buyer knows that the S.E.C. cleared the issue, he is apt to believe that the S.E.C. has endorsed it — and anything that is good enough for the S.E.C. is good enough for him.

Nothing, of course, could be further from the truth. Full disclosure can protect against fraud. It can't guarantee a profit or protect against loss. *Caveat emptor* — "let the buyer beware" — is still the rule of the market, and it applies with particular force to new, unseasoned issues.

Chapter 7

What Are Government and Municipal Bonds?

THE *government bond* poses an interesting paradox. Here is the one security about which more people know something than they do about any other. And yet here is the one security which is fully understood by probably fewer people than any other.

An estimated 85,000,000 Americans learned what it meant to lend their money on a bond, with the promise of repayment and the assurance of interest, during World War II when they bought the famous Series E bonds, and there are still other millions whose education in investments has been initiated by buying these savings bonds since the war.

But only the big institutional buyers of government bonds plus a comparative handful of dealers, who regularly buy and sell hundreds of millions of these securities for a profit measured in fractions of 1 per cent, really understand the government bond market and know how it can be affected by subtle shifts in the credit and money policies of our own government or another government half the world away.

There are dozens and dozens of different government issues,

carrying different coupon rates, different maturities, different call provisions.

Some are issued for very short periods of time. These are *government bills* with maturities as short as 91 days, *certificates* ranging up to a year, and *notes* that may run up to five years. On these short-term issues, interest rates generally range around 1% or 2%, though during World War II the government pegged the interest rates on bills at a low of ⅜ of 1%.

In contrast, long-term bonds, known as *Treasuries,* usually have maturities of fifteen or twenty years and characteristically pay about 2½% or 2¾%, though in World War I interest rates were as high as 4¼%.

On some bonds, the interest which the owner receives is partially exempt from federal taxation, but no such exemption exists on any bonds issued since March 1941.

Some of the Treasuries sell at premium prices and some below par.

These bonds, representing the great bulk of the federal debt, are always freely traded in the market at prices which change only slightly from day to day, rarely as much as a quarter or a half point. As a matter of fact, so close is this market usually that the minimum price fluctuation on government bonds is only 1/32 of a point — occasionally even 1/64 — as compared with ⅛ of a point on stocks.

Regularly traded by the same dealers and on much the same basis as the government bonds are those bonds issued by various government agencies such as the Federal Home Loan Corp. and the Federal Land Bank.

But there are other government bonds which are not

traded in any market. Bonds that can be bought only from the government and sold back to the government at set prices. Bonds that never suffer any fluctuations in market price. These are the *savings bonds — Series E, H, J, and K* — and they can be bought at virtually any bank or brokerage office. No commission is charged; they are handled free as a patriotic service.

In 1952, the government undertook to make its savings bonds more attractive by increasing their yields. Prior to that time, if you bought a $100 E bond, you paid $75 for it and got $100 back ten years later. That meant you earned an interest rate of 2.9% if you held the bond to maturity and less if you cashed it in earlier. The new E bonds can be redeemed in nine years and eight months, which means that the owner gets a full 3% interest at that time.

When this change was made, the government also introduced a new companion bond for the small investor known as Series H. If you buy a $500 Series H bond, the smallest denomination available, you pay the full $500 for it, and the government pays you interest on it semiannually. These payments are so graduated that if you hold the bond for nine years and eight months, you also earn a 3% interest on it over the full period. No person can buy more than $20,000 worth of E bonds and $20,000 of H bonds in any one year.

Anyone who wants more savings bonds — up to $200,000 worth on the issue price in any one year — can take his choice of Series J or K, which replace the old Series F and G bonds and pay a higher rate of interest.

The Series J bond is a discount bond like Series E. A $1000

J Bond costs $720 and can be redeemed twelve years later at the full $1000, which means that anyone who holds it to maturity earns an interest of 2.76%. If it is cashed in before maturity, its redemption value is less and so consequently is the actual interest rate you earn on it.

Series K bonds have a kind of insurance feature about them. These bonds are sold at the full $1000 price and carry an interest rate of 2.76%. Obviously there would be no incentive for the owner to hold the bond for the full twelve years if he could get his $27.60 yearly and sell the bond back to the government any time for $1000. So the government has worked out a system whereby the redemption value of the bond drops for the first four years to a low of $966 and then after that year slowly increases until at the end of twelve years it becomes worth $1000 again. However, the full face value is payable at any time in the event of the owner's death.

Despite all the differences between various issues, government bonds have one common characteristic: they are regarded as the safest investments in the world.

What security lies behind them? The pledged word of the Government of the United States. Just that. Nothing else. As long as that word is believed and accepted — as it must be by all Americans, since we *are* the government in the last analysis — government bonds, if held to maturity, offer the best protection you can find against the risk of losing any of your capital.

But because their prices do not rise in an inflation, they offer poor protection against the risk that your dollars will lose something of their purchasing power if prices generally go up. People who paid $75 for an E bond in 1940 got $100 back in 1950, but it would buy only about $60 worth of goods in terms of 1940 prices.

Like the federal government, states, cities, and other units of local government need capital — to build schools, roads, hospitals, and sewers, and to carry on all the many other public projects which are their responsibility. So they too issue bonds, and these are called *municipal bonds*.

Unlike the federal government which underwrites its own bonds, these local units of government go to the investment bankers for their money, just as a corporation does, and the banker underwrites municipal bond issues in very much the way that corporate bonds are underwritten and sold.

There are tens of thousands of municipal bond issues on the market. In the depression, interest rates on these bonds ran as high as 4% or 5%, but in recent years the rates have been more than cut in half. Some new issues have been brought out at even less than 1%. Most municipals are serial bonds; some are paid off in only a few years, some run for many.

No one can hope to know all about the different characteristics, the different qualities of municipal bonds, but in the main they offer the investor a fair degree of safety, and consequently their prices are more stable than stocks though less stable than government bonds. They are "safe" because the word of any unit of government, like the word of the federal government, can generally be accepted. Then too, in most municipal bonds, the revenue that is raised from specific taxes is pledged to the payment of interest on the bonds and to the repayment of the loan over a period of years.

Municipal bonds are bought by banks, fire and casualty insurance companies, estates, and many wealthy individuals. They have special appeal for the man in a high-income bracket because he doesn't have to pay a federal tax on the interest he gets from a municipal bond, as he must on the dividends which he gets as a stockholder or on the interest payments he collects from corporate bonds or most government bonds. Thus, under the tax laws, at least as they existed in 1952, a single man earning around $50,000 a year could get the same net return on a *tax-exempt* municipal bond paying 2% as he could on a stock that paid a dividend three or four times as large, and comparatively speaking, he took no risk.

This is as near as you can get in the investment business to having your cake and eating it too. All you need is a $50,000 income.

Chapter 8
How Are Securities Bought and Sold?

THE stocks of the biggest and best-known corporations in America are bought and sold on the *New York Stock Exchange*. On all but the dullest days a million shares — often two million or more — change hands there. They might be worth forty million or a hundred and forty million dollars.

That much money has a lot of glamour about it. It builds its own folklore. As a consequence, the Stock Exchange has become one of the most publicized institutions in the world, the very symbol of American capitalism.

But somehow that publicity has got in the way of public understanding — so much so that the Stock Exchange could almost be described as the business nobody knows. The business nobody knows but everybody talks about.

A lot of people, probably most people, think the Stock Exchange sells stock. It doesn't. It doesn't own any, doesn't sell any, doesn't buy any. If stocks lose a million dollars in value, the Exchange doesn't get a nickel of it. It is simply a market place where thousands of people buy and sell stocks every day, through their agents, the *brokers*.

Nor does the Stock Exchange have anything to do with fixing the price at which any of those stocks is bought and sold. The prices are arrived at in a two-way *auction* system: the buyer competes with other buyers for the lowest price, and the seller competes with other sellers for the highest price. Hence, the Stock Exchange can boast that it's the freest free market in the world, the one in which there's the least impediment to the free interplay of supply and demand. It's the very essence of free competition.

When the buyer with the highest bid and the seller with the lowest offering price conclude a transaction, each can be sure that he got the best price he could at that moment. As buyer or seller, you may not be wholly satisfied, but you can't blame the Stock Exchange any more than you can blame the weatherman if it's too hot or too cold for you.

Perhaps you've heard that the stock market is "rigged," that big operators drive prices up or hammer them down to suit themselves and make a profit at the little fellow's expense. Yes, there are some classic stories like that, and they *were* true, especially in the last century but even as recently as the nineteen-twenties when big market operators resorted to all kinds of questionable devices to *manipulate* stock prices to their own advantage.

But that isn't permitted today, and it hasn't been for some time — not since Congress outlawed such practices in 1934 and empowered the Securities & Exchange Commission to crack down on violations. That's a responsibility — just one of many — that the S.E.C. takes seriously. It has men who keep their eyes glued to the stock ticker tape every minute of the day, looking for suspicious price jiggles, anything which suggests that the freedom of the market is being tampered with.

No less zealous is the Stock Exchange in policing its own self-imposed rules to prevent sharp practices — rules that were drastically tightened when the Exchange was completely reorganized in the thirties.

Probably no business in the world operates under more stringent regulation or with a stricter code of ethics — all of it designed for the protection of buyers and sellers.

In 1934, Congress even undertook to protect the buyer of securities (and the seller too) against himself — against his own greed and rashness. Up to that time, you could buy securities with only a small down payment or *margin*. Typically it was 20%. Often it was less. And an occasional customer even "bought" securities 100% on credit — without putting up a dime. That's how a few people made a fortune on a shoestring, but it's also how more of them brought disaster on themselves and thousands of others in the 1929 crash.

Nowadays, the Federal Reserve Board decides what the minimum down payment shall be, and its decision is binding on everybody. The Board changes the figure from time to time. Since 1934, it has ranged from as low as 40% of the purchase price up to 100%, and when the 100% rule prevailed that meant there was no credit at all; the buyer had to pay in full for his stocks.

This power alone — the power of the Reserve Board to say what the minimum margin shall be — guarantees that there will never be another market crash quite like 1929. Stock prices are bound to go down from time to time and down sharply. Indeed, in 1937–1938, despite the regulatory powers of the federal government, they dropped about 50% in just eight months. But it can still be said that the market can never crash as spectacularly as it did in 1929, when it began the big slide down to the 1932 low, a drop that saw stocks lose on the average almost 90% of their value.

That can't happen again because under the Reserve Board's margin regulation, prices can never be as overinflated as they were when people bought hundreds of millions of stocks by putting up only a fraction of that amount in cash.

One noteworthy result of all the regulations that have been imposed on the market has been a change in the character of the market itself. It has become more of an investor's market, less of a speculator's market. Of course, speculators still buy and sell stocks in the hopes of making a profit, and this function is not only legitimate but useful and desirable in the main, because it helps provide a continuous and liquid market. It helps stabilize prices, thus permitting the investor to buy and sell more readily and at fairer prices.

Nevertheless, more of the people who buy stocks today are doing so for the sake of earning a good return on their money over the long pull. They are not *"in-and-outers,"* people trading for a small profit on every market move. Generally, they hold their stocks for years and years. They're investors — people who want to be part owners of those "biggest and best-known corporations."

All told, on the New York Stock Exchange, the securities of about 1100 of these companies have been *listed*, which means that they have been accepted for trading there. To qualify, a company has to meet certain requirements, which have become more exacting over the years.

For one thing, when a company applies for listing, it must have substantial assets and be able to show that it earned at least a million dollars in the preceding year. All told, in a typical year, the listed companies usually account for about half of all the net profits and two thirds of all dividend payments reported by American companies.

Furthermore, the company must be able to show that enough people have an interest in its stock to assure a good market for it. Today, the Exchange will not list a stock unless the company has at least 1500 stockholders and at least 300,000 shares of stock outstanding. Most companies exceed these requirements by a wide margin. American Telephone & Telegraph has the greatest number of stockholders — over 1,200,-000 — and General Motors with 88,000,000 shares has the largest amount of stock outstanding. All told, more than two and a half billion shares are listed on the Exchange.

A company must also agree to publish quarterly reports of its financial condition, as certified by independent accountants. In the old days, only annual reports were required, and some companies were admitted on these terms. Nevertheless, about 90% of all listed companies now report quarterly.

Finally, a company must agree not to issue any additional shares without Exchange approval, and it must have a *registrar* in New York City to see that no more shares of stock are issued than the company has a right to sell. It must also have a *transfer agent* who keeps an exact record of all stockholders, their names, addresses, and number of shares owned.

The companies whose stocks and bonds are traded on the Exchange have nothing to say about its operation. The brokers run their own show, although the paid president must be a man who has no connection with the securities business and the 33-man *Board of Governors* must contain three public members who have no identification with the securities business.

Legally, the Exchange isn't a corporation or even a partnership. It's nothing but a voluntary association of individual members whose number in 1952 totaled 1375.

The business of trading in stocks in New York goes back to the early eighteenth century when merchants and auctioneers used to congregate at the foot of Wall Street to buy and sell not only stocks but wheat, tobacco, and other commodities, including slaves.

In 1792, two dozen merchants who used to meet daily under a buttonwood tree on Wall Street and trade various stocks agreed from then on to deal only with each other and to charge their customers a fixed commission. Thus began the New York Stock Exchange, the first organized securities exchange in America.

How do you become a member of this association today? If you are approved by the Exchange Board of Governors you buy a *seat*. Since nobody but a postman is on his feet more continuously than a broker, that is one of the classic misnomers of our language. It had its origin in the leisurely days of 1793 when the new association took up quarters in the Tontine Coffee House.

What does a seat cost? That depends on how good business

is on the Exchange. In 1929, three different seats were sold at $625,000 each, an all-time high. Later the number of seats was increased 25%, so no one of them was worth quite as much, but it is hard to believe they could fall to the low they hit in 1942 when one was sold for $17,000, which is less than the amount regularly given as a gift to the family of a member on his death by the rest of the members. In recent years, seats have recovered some of their former value, but in 1952 when the Exchange considered a proposal to reduce its membership by fifty seats, it expected to be able to buy in those seats at a maximum price of $45,000.

A handful of the seats, about thirty of them, are owned by men who aren't really brokers at all. They are *floor traders,* men who buy and sell stocks wholly for themselves. Because they pay no commissions, by virtue of their membership in the Exchange, they are able to make money by taking small speculative profits on a few transactions every day. But this has become more difficult, because of the increase in taxes that are levied on stock transactions, small as they are. Furthermore the traders must operate under very severe regulations imposed by the Exchange to see that they have no possible advantage over the public. As a result, their number has decreased and so has their activity. Today the traders account for only 2% or 3% of all transactions.

All the other brokers earn their living handling orders for the public, some directly and some indirectly. Over 600 of the memberships are held by various partners in the *brokerage firms* that buy and sell stocks for the public. These firms operate about 1700 branch offices in well over 400 cities here

and abroad. In still other cities they are represented by corre-
spondents — almost 3000 of them. Usually these correspond-
ents are local security dealers or banks.

Some 500,000 miles of private or leased telephone and teletype wires keep all of the offices of these brokerage firms, the
so-called *wire houses,* in almost instantaneous touch with the
Exchange, and as a result the man who may live only a mile
or two away from the Exchange has no advantage over the
man who lives 3000 miles away.

Chapter 9
What Does It Cost to Buy Stocks?

SINCE the New York Stock Exchange began, the brokers who are members have charged standard minimum *commissions* on the orders that they execute to buy or sell stocks for others.

How much are these commissions?

They vary with the price of the stock and the number of shares bought. But on almost any purchase or sale, the commission is a great deal less than you probably imagine. This is so because most people think in terms of the 5% commission that a real estate broker usually charges on the sale of property. In contrast, the commission charged on stocks averages out to only about 1% on all orders executed on the New York Stock Exchange over a period of a year.

Here is the basic schedule of rates effective November 9, 1953.

On a purchase or sale amounting to $100 or less: As mutually agreed, usually around 6%.

On a purchase or sale between $100 and $999.99: 1% plus $5.

On a purchase or sale from $1000 to $3999.99: ½ of 1%, plus $15.

On a purchase or sale amounting to $4000 or more: 1/10 of 1%, plus $35.

These rates apply on the purchase or sale of 100 shares of a given stock. If you buy or sell less than 100 shares, you are permitted a $2 reduction in these rates, but you will have to pay extra costs on such small orders (see Chapter 12); so the $2 reduction is not clear profit.

If you sell a stock within 15 days after buying it, the commission on the sale is reduced to 50% of the regular amount plus $2.50 for a 100-share unit or $1.50 for less than 100 shares.

Regardless of how much money is involved in any transaction, no commission can exceed $1 a share or $50 per 100 shares.

There is also a standard scale of commissions for corporate bonds traded on the New York Stock Exchange — $5 apiece for one or two bonds, $4 each on three bonds, $3 each on four bonds, and $2.50 apiece on five or more bonds.

Since only members of the Exchange can execute orders there, other security dealers must turn all regular commission orders for listed securities over to some member for execution. This means that if you give an order to a nonmember, such as a bank or a security dealer, you may have to pay an additional fee. No member broker is permitted to split commissions with a nonmember.

In addition to a commission, you will also have to pay *transfer taxes* levied by New York State and the federal government every time you sell a stock. The New York State tax ranges between 1¢ and 4¢ a share, depending on the price of the stock; the higher-priced stocks pay the higher tax.

The federal tax is based on par value. On a stock selling at less than $20 a share, the seller must pay 5¢ on every $100 of par value represented by the shares he sells. Thus, if you sell 100 shares, at a price of $19 per share, of a stock that has a $10 par value, you would pay a federal tax of 50¢, since your shares would represent $1000 of par value. If your stock sells at more than $20 a share, the tax rate is 6¢ per $100 of par value. Thus, if you sold the same shares at $21, your federal tax would be 60¢.

A good many companies have abandoned par value because it bears no real relationship to the actual value of stock, and they have consequently issued stock of no par value. The federal government has met this problem by ruling that all no-par stock shall be assumed to have a value of $100 a share. That's one reason why so many companies have put the par value of their stock at $1 or $5 a share.

Both these federal and state taxes are levied on the seller. However, if you buy less than 100 shares of a listed stock you must pay the federal tax.

Finally, to cover the costs incurred by the Securities & Exchange Commission in its regulatory work, a small added fee is levied on all stock sales. It amounts to only 1¢ on every $500 worth of stock.

(On corporate bonds, the seller pays a federal tax of 50¢ but no New York State tax; government and municipal bonds are wholly tax-free.)

Since most of the large brokerage firms are headquartered in New York City, and since New York like all other cities is anxious to tap every source of revenue, Father Knickerbocker has also been eying the securities business hungrily. Some years ago, the city government first levied a tax of 2/10 of 1% on the gross commissions earned by brokers. Then the tax was increased to $\frac{4}{10}$ of 1%. And in 1952, presumably for a one-year emergency period only, the tax was increased to $\frac{8}{10}$ of 1%. This city tax is paid by the brokers and cannot be passed along to the buyer or seller of securities, but it does represent a big increase in the broker's cost of doing business and does make any proposal for an increase in their commission rates look more attractive.

Whenever this question of a rate increase comes up, the New York Stock Exchange is a house divided. The smaller brokers who may deal principally with a few big customers are usually in favor of a rate increase on the smaller transactions that they may have to handle frequently at a loss. On the other hand, the big wire houses that deal with a broader segment of the public are usually not so well disposed to a rate increase, and if one has to be made, they are likely to feel that it should fall primarily on those best able to pay it, not on the little man whom they want to interest in investing.

The big brokers, too, may lose money on some small orders, but since the redistribution of wealth in this country inevitably means that there will be more rather than fewer small buyers, they are constantly attempting to step up the efficiency of their operations so that they will be able to handle such business profitably. Then, too, they can always hope that the small buyer will someday become a bigger investor.

Chapter 10
How the Stock Exchange Works

WHAT actually happens on the New York Stock Exchange when a broker gets an order to buy or sell stock? How is the transaction completed with another broker so that both buyer and seller are assured of the best price possible at that moment?

Consider first the physical layout of the Stock Exchange. It is a big building at the corner of Wall and Broad Streets in New York City. The trading room looks something like an armory with a high ceiling and a trading floor about half the size of a football field.

All around the edge of the *trading floor* are "*telephone booths.*" These booths bear no resemblance to any others that you have ever seen. They are open at both ends, and along the two sides there are spaces at which about twenty clerks, each representing an individual broker, can work. At each clerk's space, above the narrow counter at which he stands and does his endless paper work, there are telephones connecting him with his home office. These phones are the nerve ends of the securities business, for it is through them that virtually all the public orders to buy or sell stocks come to the floor of the Exchange.

Spaced at regular intervals on the trading floor are 18 *trading posts,* 12 on the main trading floor and 6 in the "garage" or annex. Each trading post or station is a horseshoe-shaped counter, occupying about 100 square feet of floor space. Behind the counter inside the station, there is room for a dozen other clerks and for several paid employees of the Exchange.

All buying and selling is done around the outside of the trading post. About 70 different stocks are bought and sold at each post, at different positions around the perimeter, a half dozen or so at each position.

Little placards on a board above the open counter show just which stocks are sold at each position, and below each placard is a price indicator showing the last price at which a transaction in that stock took place and whether this price represented an increase or decrease from the last different price — a plus sign if it represented an increase, a minus sign for a decrease.

When an order is received at the headquarters office of any brokerage firm in New York City, it is phoned over to the clerk in that firm's booth. Some firms have booth space for only two or three clerks, and one big wire house has 35 spaces in half a dozen booths.

When the clerk receives an order over the phone, he writes it out and hands it to the floor broker, because only members can trade on the floor. If the broker is not at the booth, the clerk can summon him simply by pushing a button. Every broker has a number, and when the clerk pushes the button, the broker's number is flashed on a large annunciator board at each end of the trading room. If the clerk knows his broker is busy with other orders, he employs the services of a so-called $2 *broker*.

There are about 200 of these men who own their own seats on the Exchange and make their living by transacting business for the wire houses. The $2 broker got his name in the days when he received that fee for every order that he executed. Nowadays he is compensated on a sliding scale, which ranges from 50¢ to $4.00 per order executed. In the average case, he makes about $3 on every order he handles. This is called a *floor give-up commission,* for the obvious reason that the broker who is responsible for the order gives up a part of his commission to the broker who actually executes the order.

Let's assume that with the passage of years, the Rod & Reel Co. has grown to the point where its stock is listed on the New York Stock Exchange, and that the order which the clerk gives his broker is a market order to buy 100 shares of Rod & Reel. A *market order* is one to be executed as soon as feasible at the best price the broker can get. As soon as the broker has the written order in his hand, he walks over to the exact position outside the trading post where he knows other brokers with orders to buy or sell Rod & Reel will come.

As he approaches the post, he looks at the price indicator and notes that the last sale of Rod & Reel took place at 18¾, which means $18.75 a share. However, some broker may now be willing to sell it for less than that price, and so as he enters the "crowd" of the other brokers at the trading position — two, three, or a dozen of them, however many are interested in buying or selling Rod & Reel right then — he simply asks, "How's Reel?" He doesn't disclose whether he wants to buy or sell; he simply asks the question. Another broker in the crowd may answer, "Eighteen and three eighths to eighteen

66

and three fourths," or simply, "Three eighths to three fourths." This means that 18⅜ is the best bid, the most any broker is then willing to pay, and 18¾ the best offer, the lowest anyone will sell for.

Our broker will try to get the stock cheaper if he can; so he waits a few seconds for other offers. Finally he decides to tip his hand and make a bid. So he says, "One half for one hundred," by which he means that he will pay $18.50 a share for 100 shares.

If he gets no response, he may raise his bid by ⅛ of a point. This is the minimum fluctuation in the price of most stocks. So, he announces, "Five eighths for one hundred." At this point perhaps the first broker who offered the stock at 18¾ may have decided that he can't get that price. Or another broker, who may have entered the crowd later, will decide to accept this bid of 18⅝. If either one of them decides to "hit" the bid, he says "Sold" and the transaction is concluded, simply on the basis of that spoken word. Conversely, if a broker decides to accept an offering price announced in the course of an auction, he simply says, "I'll take it." No written memoranda are exchanged by the brokers.

The rules of the New York Stock Exchange provide that all bids to buy and all offers to sell must be made by open outcry. No secret transactions are permitted on the floor of the Exchange. Furthermore, a broker cannot conclude transactions between his own customers without presenting their orders to buy and sell on the floor. For instance, he may have a market order to buy 100 shares of Rod & Reel and another order to sell 100 at the market. He can't just "*cross*" these orders privately and effect a transfer of the stock between his two customers. He must send both orders to the floor where the appropriate bids and offers must be made. Only in very rare cases are off-the-market crosses permitted, and even in these cases, both buyer and seller must know that the transfer is being so negotiated and the Stock Exchange must grant permission for such a transaction.

No broker is permitted to execute any orders except during the official trading hours of the Exchange. These are from 10 A.M. to 3:30 P.M. Monday through Friday, excepting holidays.

As soon as a transaction such as the Rod & Reel purchase at 18⅝ is completed, the broker who bought the stock and the broker who sold it make their own separate records of the transaction. After the close of the market, their two firms will arrange for the actual transfer of the stock and the payment of the amount due. Actually, these two firms might have concluded many transactions with each other in the course of the day, and in turn, each of them might have dealt with dozens of other brokers.

All settlements between member firms are arranged through the New York Stock Exchange Clearing Corporation, so that a minimum of cash and securities are exchanged. Thus, a firm may have sold 1100 shares of Rod & Reel for its customers on a given day and bought only 1000. To settle its accounts in that stock on that day, the firm would have to send only 100 shares to the Clearing Corporation. The delivery of the other 1000 shares from its own customers who sold that stock to those customers who bought it is purely an internal bookkeeping

68

procedure. Dollar balances, the net amounts owed and the net amounts due, are handled in the same way.

After the sale of Rod & Reel took place at 18⅝, one of the four or five *floor reporters,* who stand outside each trading post, would see that the price indicator on the post was changed — from 18¾ to 18⅝. And since this sale was below the preceding sale, he would be sure that a minus sign showed beside the price figure.

He would also write a report of the sale — the name of the stock, the number of shares involved, and the price. This report would be handed to a page boy, who would take it to the pneumatic tubes that lead directly from each post to the ticker room. There a notation of the sale would be typed onto the *ticker tape,* and it would be carried by wire to the *tickers* in every broker's office throughout the country.

On the tape the name of every stock appears only as initials or a combination of letters, such as C for Chrysler Corp., CP for Canadian Pacific, and CGW for Chicago Great Western. The single-letter symbols are, of course, the most highly prized and the best known. Thus A stands for Anaconda, C for Chrysler, M for Montgomery Ward, N for International Nickel, T for American Telephone & Telegraph and, most famous of them all, X for U.S. Steel.

Rod & Reel might have the symbol RAR and the transaction would appear on the tape simply as:

RAR 18⅝

If 200 shares instead of 100 shares had changed hands, the transaction would be noted this way:

RAR 2s 18⅝

If 1000 shares had been involved, it would appear on the tape this way:

RAR 1000s 18⅝

When sales volume is so heavy that the ticker — the highest-speed printer in the world — falls as much as one minute behind, the price information is abbreviated to the last digit plus a fraction, except when that digit is a zero as in 20 or 30. If the ticker were late, our sale at 18⅝ would appear as

RAR 8⅝

It is assumed that people who are following the stock closely on the ticker will be able to supply the missing first digit. Of course, if the stock were to go up to 20 or above, this price would be noted in full, such as 20⅛.

The ticker rarely falls as much as five minutes behind the market, but sometimes this does happen. In such situations, to keep traders abreast of the market action, the Exchange resorts to *flash* printing, and at half-minute intervals it flashes the latest prices of 30 key stocks representing a variety of industries on the tape. These up-to-the-second price announcements are always preceded by the word "flash," and no volume figure is given. Whenever the tape recovers lost time, it returns to usual routines.

When most people think of buying or selling stock they think of doing it on the basis of a market order, one to be executed as soon as possible after it reaches the floor and at the best price then prevailing. Actually, an individual very often wants to buy or sell a stock only if it can be done at a certain price or better. Thus, you might want to buy 100 shares of Rod & Reel provided you didn't have to pay more than 18½. You could place an order to this effect with your broker. It's called a *limit order,* and you can tell him whether it's good for a day, a week, a month, or "good till canceled."

The stock will be bought for you only if it can be bought at 18½ or less. Perhaps when the order is actually executed, your broker will be able to get the stock at 18¼. On the other hand, the stock may actually drop to 18½, and your order won't have been filled. That's because other orders to buy at 18½ were placed ahead of yours, and the supply of the stock offered at that price was exhausted before your order was reached. In that kind of situation, if you asked your broker why your order wasn't executed, he would tell you that there was *"stock ahead."*

Limit orders can also be used in selling stock. Thus, if you owned Rod & Reel stock, you might be willing to sell it but only if you could get $19 for it — $19 or more. You could place a sell limit order to that effect with your broker.

There's still another kind of suspended buying order and this is known as the *stop-loss order* or just *stop order.*

Suppose you had bought Rod & Reel at 12 or 13, and the stock had risen to a level where you had a nice profit — perhaps to 19 or 20. You might want to protect that profit in case the market dropped sharply, and you could do so by instructing your broker to sell the stock if it declined to, let's say, 18. This would be a stop-loss order, and your broker would see that it was executed if Rod & Reel ever fell as low as 18. Whenever it hit that mark, your stop order would become a market order to be executed at the best price then possible. Again, because other people might have placed advance orders to sell at that figure, the price might slip to 17¾ or 17½ before your order could be executed.

In theory these fixed-price orders, both limit orders and stop-loss orders, look pretty attractive as a means of controlling your profits or losses. In practice, however, they don't work as well for the average investor as you might think. To have any real utility, a limit order has to be pretty close to the prevailing market price. For instance, if Rod & Reel is selling at 18½, there might not be much point in placing an order to buy it at 16 or even 17. And if you place a limit order at 18, you might just as well buy it outright at 18½. If you don't, you might never get another chance to buy it so cheaply. The price might rise to 19 or 20, and go right on up. The same logic applies in selling a stock.

In short, decisions to buy or sell that turn on getting an extra fraction of a point profit are not apt to be sound decisions for the average investor.

Chapter 11
How a Market Is Made

WHENEVER you place an order with a broker, he is responsible for seeing that it is executed at the best price possible, the best as far as your interests are concerned. Often this would require him to spend far more time on your order than he can afford to spare if he is to see that all his other orders are also properly executed. Thus, for instance, if you were to place a limit order to buy Rod & Reel at 18 or better when that stock was selling at 18½, you could hardly expect your broker to spend all his time keeping an eye on Rod & Reel, waiting to see if it dropped to 18.

In a case like that, he would turn your order over to another broker who, as his agent, would watch the stock for you and execute the order if he could. This agent would be the *specialist* in Rod & Reel stock.

A specialist is a broker who has elected to confine his activities to a particular group of stocks sold at one spot around the perimeter of a trading post. He never moves away from that spot; he is always there to accept orders from other brokers and, for a fee, to assume responsibility for their execution.

All told, there are about 350 specialists who handle the stocks of the 1100 companies listed on the Exchange. Some specialists, together with one or more partners, may handle dozens of stocks, and some have only a couple. In some active stocks like General Motors or U.S. Steel there are as many as three specialists, each competing with the others.

No broker can operate as a specialist except with the approval of the Stock Exchange, and his operations are closely regulated both by the Exchange and the S.E.C.

A specialist must not only function as an agent for other brokers, executing the orders that they leave with him, but he must also be willing to buy and sell for his own account the stocks in which he specializes.

When a commission broker comes to the trading post with an order to sell a stock and there are no other brokers with buy orders for that stock at the post, the specialist will make a bid for the stock himself. Similarly, when a broker wants to buy a stock and there are no other sellers, the specialist will offer it for sale himself. About 10% of Stock Exchange volume results from this kind of buying and selling by specialists for their own accounts.

On each of the stocks in which he specializes, the specialist keeps a book, and in this book he enters all the orders that other brokers give him to be executed. These orders are entered in his book chronologically, and those that are received first are executed first, whenever the price auction permits, regardless of all other conditions or circumstances.

Thus, if your order for Rod & Reel at 18 were the first one in the specialist's book, and if the stock were offered at that price, your order would be filled first. Even if he wanted to, the specialist couldn't buy the stock for his own account at 18 until your order and all others in his book at that price were executed. For handling such transactions, the specialist gets the same floor give-up commission as the $2 broker.

Whenever the last sale of Rod & Reel was made at 18½, the specialist's book might typically show one or two limit orders to buy at 18⅜, one or two others at 18¼, perhaps three or four at 18, since most customers place limit orders in round figures rather than fractions. On the sell side, his book might show a couple of orders to sell at 18⅝, a few at 18¾, and several at 19 or higher. These might be either limit orders or stop-loss orders, and would be so marked in his book.

In that situation if a broker came to the trading post with a market order to buy Rod & Reel and there were no other brokers there with stock to sell, his query, "How's Reel?" would be answered by the specialist. The specialist would reply, "Three eighths — five eighths," meaning 18⅜ bid and 18⅝ offered, since 18⅜ was the highest buy order and 18⅝ the lowest sell order that he then had in his book. This would be the *bid-and-asked* quotation as of then.

In the case of a typical stock the difference between the bid and offering prices is usually only ¼ or ½ point. If the difference is more than that, the specialist, under the rules of the Exchange, would be expected to narrow the difference by making the appropriate bids or offers on his own and buying or selling the stock for his own account as necessary.

In the handling of market orders when there are no other brokers to participate in the auction, the specialist performs another important service, which is called *"stopping a stock."*

Suppose your broker came to the trading post with your market order for Rod & Reel when the best offering price

in the specialist's book was 18⅝ and when there were no
other brokers there with better offers. Anxious to get a better price for you if possible, and yet not wanting to miss the
market if it were to go up, your broker would ask the specialist to stop 100 shares for him at 18⅝. If another broker
were to come up then and offer Rod & Reel at 18½, the specialist would buy it for your broker and earn a give-up commission.
On the other hand, if the stock were not offered at a lower
price but sold again the next time at 18⅝, the specialist would
execute your buy order at that figure. He could not execute
your order at more than 18⅝, for when he was asked to stop
the stock, he agreed to sell it at that maximum price.

After every sale a wholly new auction starts. Thus, if a
transaction in Rod & Reel had just been concluded at 18⅝,
other brokers in the crowd who might be trying to buy 100
shares apiece would immediately restate their bids, probably
the same bid — 18½. If there were no order on the specialist's book that had a clearly established time priority, these
three simultaneous bids would have parity, and if a broker
then came up and offered the stock at 18½, the three brokers
who wanted to buy at that price would settle the matter as
to which one would get the stock by tossing a coin.

The brokers who lost out might then report to their customers that they had "*matched and lost.*" Customers who get
such a report often wonder why they never win. The answer
is that the broker never reports when he matches and wins;
the customer simply gets the stock.

In the case of simultaneous bids, if one broker has an order
for 200 shares while the others are trying to buy only 100

shares apiece, the larger order takes precedence if the seller offers a block that big or bigger. If the seller offered 200 shares, the broker who wanted 200 would get it all. If the seller had 300 shares, the broker who wanted the 200 would get his first, and the other two would have to match for the remaining 100.

Very often, before placing a market order, a customer wants to have a pretty exact idea of what he might have to pay. To accommodate such a customer, the floor broker will try to "get the *market and the size*." This means that he will ask the specialist for the current bid-and-asked prices and how big the orders are at these prices. The specialist will tell him only the highest bid and the lowest offer, such as on Rod & Reel, "Three eighths — five eighths," or $18\frac{3}{8}$ bid, offered at $18\frac{5}{8}$. He is not permitted to reveal any of the lower bids or higher offering prices shown on his book. As far as the size of the orders is concerned, he might say, "One hundred either way," by which he would mean that he has 100 shares to buy at $18\frac{3}{8}$ and 100 to sell at $18\frac{5}{8}$. If he had 100 to buy and 500 to sell, he would say, "Three eighths — five eighths, one hundred to five hundred."

The specialist is not required to divulge the size of the orders on his book if he feels that it would not be in the best interests of the customers.

Quotations can also be obtained from the Stock Exchange's *Quotation Bureau*. The specialists at the trading post are responsible for seeing that the Quotation Bureau is advised of every change in the quotes, and any broker who subscribes to the Quotation Bureau service can get the latest quotation simply by phoning the Bureau. He cannot, however, get the size of the orders over the phone.

Because many people think the specialist has inside information about the market for the stocks he handles, he has often been accused of using that special knowledge for his personal advantage. And that's why there has been a demand from time to time that the Securities & Exchange Commission or the Exchange abolish his function and institute a system under which the specialist would be permitted to keep the book and execute orders as a broker or agent, but not to buy or sell for his own account.

After an exhaustive investigation, the S.E.C. concluded that specialists, who usually execute more than half the orders on the Exchange, rendered a useful service. More importantly, the Commission turned up no evidence of price manipulation. As a matter of fact, it found that during the period of its study, the specialist traded more often against the daily trend of prices than with it. He sold when others bought and bought when they sold. Thus he helped to stabilize price fluctuations.

Specialists operate under very strict rules — their trading accounts are regularly audited by the Exchange — and regulations are such that any violation of trust on a specialist's part would involve heavy penalties, such as suspension or even expulsion.

Certainly on many an occasion the specialist is called upon to carry a very considerable burden of risk in order to maintain an orderly market in his stocks. This is obviously the case in a declining market, and it is especially true when some important news break may seriously affect the price of his stocks, stocks that he may own himself in substantial quantity.

For instance, if a company suffered some serious setback, such as destruction of its plant, the specialist might be suddenly confronted with so many orders to sell the stock and so many cancellations of buy orders in his book that there would, in effect, be no market for the stock — just sellers and no buyers. Prices would plunge rapidly down.

In such a situation, the specialist would attempt to develop buying orders from the floor traders or other specialists. If the price break were more than 2 points on a stock selling over 10, or 1 point on a stock below 10, he would be required to consult with one of the Stock Exchange governors about what would constitute a fair market, and he would then announce the price at which he personally would buy the stock and the price at which he would sell it. As trading developed later, his judgment could be proved either sound and profitable for him or bad and costly.

When a customer wants to buy or sell a large block of stock he can tell his broker to use his own best judgment about how to execute that order to get the best possible price. This kind of order presents a ticklish problem. Suppose a broker has such an order to sell 1000 shares of a stock and offers the whole block at once. That offer might very well depress the price appreciably. On the other hand, if he feeds the stock out, a hundred shares at a time, he might fare no better. In a falling market, he might fare even worse.

Time was when a broker in that situation could turn the order over to the specialist to execute on a *"not held"* basis.

On this basis the specialist would be free to exercise his own best judgment about when and how to sell the stock. He might, for instance, hold the order back in the expectation that prices would rise, but if instead they dropped before he executed the order — if other orders were filled at higher prices than he finally realized on all or part of his not-held order — he was at least assured that the broker for whom he was acting would "not hold" him to the tape, would not hold him responsible for those better intervening prices that he had missed.

The S.E.C. insists, however, that specialists cannot accept not-held orders, and this makes the handling of such orders difficult for the broker. One thing he can do is ask the customer to convert his order into a definite limit order, and the broker can then turn it over to the specialist to execute as best he can within the definite price limit set.

Occasionally, when a broker has a large block of stock to sell, he will offer it to the specialist who may buy it outright for his own account, thus assuming the entire risk that he will be able to sell it at a profit.

When brokers have very large blocks of stock to sell — ten or twenty thousand shares or more — they sometimes do it through *special offerings* subject to the approval of the Exchange. Such an offering at a stipulated price is announced to all other brokers on the ticker, and during the trading day the broker who has the offering will sell parts or all of the stock at the announced price. To stimulate buying by other brokers, an extra compensation may be paid on all orders that they generate. In this sense, a special offering is very much like an original offering of a new stock issue in which the underwriter sets the price and the commission on all sales.

A *secondary offering* is exactly like a special offering except that it is handled after the gong sounds the close of the market instead of during the trading hours, and as a consequence nonmembers can also participate. Ordinarily a stock sold in such fashion is offered at the price of the last transaction that took place in that stock on the floor during regular trading hours.

Chapter 12
How Small Orders Are Handled

ALL stocks bought and sold on the Stock Exchange are traded in units of 100 shares, with the exception of a few inactive stocks. The 100-share unit is known as a *round lot*.

But what if you want to buy or sell just 10 shares of our hypothetical Rod & Reel Company? The answer is that you can do it, and your order will be executed at exactly the same price as if it were a round lot, thanks to the services provided by a special kind of broker, who does nothing but buy and sell *odd lots,* anything from 1 share to 99 shares. You pay the regular commission (page 60), but you will also have to pay the *odd-lot broker* for his service, and he charges a standard fee of ⅛ point or 12½¢ on every share you buy or sell of a stock selling below $40 a share, and ¼ point or 25¢ on stocks shelling at $40 or above.

The odd-lot broker will not only execute market orders for you, but he will also handle limit orders. These do pose an additional problem. Since he buys stock for you at either ⅛ or ¼ above the actual market price and sells for you at ⅛ or ¼ below the market, he will not execute a limit order for you unless the price of the stock is such that it will cover his fee. Thus, if you place a limit order to buy Rod & Reel at 18½ or lower, he will not execute the order for you until the stock drops at least to 18⅜. A limit order to sell at 18½ will not be executed unless the stock reached 18⅝. If the stock were selling over $40, the differential would be ¼ instead of ⅛.

Stop orders on odd lots, however, are executed whenever the stock hits the specified price. If you place a stop order to sell Rod & Reel at 18½, it will become a market order for execution as soon as feasible whenever the stock hits that price. However, if it is executed at 18½, you will net only 18⅜ on the sale.

The odd-lot broker isn't really a broker at all. Technically, he is a *dealer*. A broker acts only as your agent; he doesn't sell anything of his own to you, and he doesn't buy anything from you. On the floor of the Exchange he simply bargains for you. In contrast, a dealer sells to you something that he himself owns when you place an order to buy; he sells it to you from his supply or inventory. Conversely, when you sell to him, he buys what you offer for his own account.

And that's what the odd-lot houses do, when they execute your stock orders. Two firms — Carlisle & Jacquelin and De Coppet & Doremus — handle over 99% of the odd-lot business on the Stock Exchange, and each of them usually has on hand a good-sized inventory of many listed stocks. Just how big an inventory depends on whether the market is going up or down, but it is likely to average about two million dollars' worth of stock. Whenever they sell more of a given stock than they buy, they must sooner or later replenish their supply by buying another 100 shares, a round lot, in a regular auction on the floor of the Exchange.

This is why the odd-lot buyer has to pay that federal transfer tax levied on sales,* and the round-lot buyer doesn't. Whenever you buy an odd lot, the dealer sells it to you, and the government has ruled that that sale is taxable; so the odd-lot dealer passes the tax on to the buyer.

To assure the odd-lot buyer the same price as the round-lot buyer, both the big odd-lot houses have brokers at every trading post. These men, over 100 of them, are not employees but regular members of the Exchange who earn their income by seeing that the odd-lot orders are properly executed.

The odd-lot firms do not deal with the public, only with other members. Consequently your market order for 10 shares of Rod & Reel must be placed through a regular member firm. When it is phoned into your broker's booth on the floor, it is marked for handling either by De Coppet & Doremus or Carlisle & Jacquelin. (Most wire houses try to split their odd-lot business pretty evenly between the two houses.)

The clerk then sends the order by pneumatic tube — there are 35 miles of such tubes in the Exchange — direct to the trading post on which Rod & Reel is sold. A page boy stamps the time at which the order is received and gives it to the odd-lot broker handling business at that post for whichever one of the two houses gets this order. The broker goes at once to the position at which Rod & Reel is sold, and when the next round lot of Rod & Reel is traded by other round-lot brokers, the price arrived at in that transaction becomes the price at which you buy your 10 shares. You get all the benefits of having participated in that auction.

* See p. 62.

After the sale, the odd-lot broker makes a report of the transaction, time-stamps the report, and sends it back by pneumatic tube to your own broker's booth.

You might ask why the odd-lot houses use brokers at all. Why couldn't the odd-lot house simply set its price on the basis of the next Rod & Reel sale reported on the ticker? The answer to that is that the odd-lot houses guarantee that they give the small investor the actual market price — the price that is made in the next round-lot auction after his order.

That actual price and the price shown on the ticker may be quite different, partly because of the delay in getting prices up to the ticker room and on the tape, partly because the tape sometimes runs late.

Arguments occasionally arise because of that very difference in prices, and that's why odd-lot orders are time-stamped as they arrive at the trading post and again as they leave. Further, the odd-lot dealers back in their offices have a clerk for each of the 18 trading posts on the floor, and each of those clerks does nothing but watch a special deleter tape which shows nothing but the trades executed on his post; all others are deleted. And that tape is also time-stamped every minute. Hence, the odd-lot firms are well prepared to answer any complaint from an odd-lot customer or his broker that his order was not executed at the proper price.

Sometimes the odd-lot trader doesn't want to wait for the next round-lot transaction. In that case, he can simply instruct his broker to buy at the lowest offering price or sell at the highest bid which either the specialist or another broker quotes when his order reaches the trading post, and the odd-lot firm will follow these instructions.

How important is the odd-lot buyer in the total market picture?

Currently he accounts for about one eighth of all the shares bought and sold on the Exchange, but because he buys in smaller units, he accounts for a quarter to a third of all individual transactions. In the last two years, he has become more important, although the odd-lot proportion of the business still lags behind what it was in the thirties or early forties.

Since the war, many popular stocks have been split on a 2-for-1, 5-for-1, or even a 10-for-1 basis, and with the consequent lowering of the per share price of such stocks, many small customers have found themselves able to buy in the more economical 100-share units. Hence, they have graduated into the round-lot end of the business.

Chapter 13
Other Exchanges — Here and in Canada

ALTHOUGH they differ somewhat in rules, regulations, and operating mechanics, the other stock exchanges in the United States, about a score of them, function fundamentally in much the same way as the New York Stock Exchange, although in a more free and easy fashion, less bound by rule and regulation.

All told, the securities of almost 4000 corporations are listed on the organized exchanges, but on the basis of the dollar value of all stocks traded about 85% of the business is done on the New York Stock Exchange — the *Big Board* as it is called — with less than one third of the listings.

The second biggest exchange is the *New York Curb Exchange,* which at the beginning of 1953 changed its name officially to the *American Stock Exchange.* This exchange accounts for another 7% or 8% of the business. Rightly or wrongly, the Curb, as it will long be known, is regarded as a kind of prep school for the New York Stock Exchange. Such important companies as General Motors and Montgomery Ward and the various Standard Oil companies had their start on the Curb.

But there are many other big companies, such as the Great

Atlantic and Pacific Tea Company, Singer Sewing Machine Company, Humble Oil, and Pepperell, which remain faithful to the Curb and have made no attempt to get their securities listed on the Big Board, even though many of them could meet the more exacting requirements there.

The Curb got its name from the fact that it actually began as a curbstone market, first on Wall and Hanover Streets in New York City and later on Broad Street. It remained an outdoor market until 1921 when it finally moved indoors, thus depriving the city of one of its most colorful spectacles. Most of the trading was done by hand signal, and orders were relayed to the brokers by shouts and whistles from offices in adjoining buildings. Even in its spacious new building, far more modern than the Stock Exchange, orders are relayed from the clerks at their phones to floor brokers by hand signals.

Seat prices on the Curb have ranged from a high of $254,000 in 1929 to a low of $650 in 1942, but by 1952 they had recovered to $13,000.

The third biggest United States exchange, the *Midwest Stock Exchange,* came into being in 1949, when the Chicago Stock Exchange undertook to effect a consolidation of its activities with those of other exchanges in Cleveland, St. Louis, and Minneapolis–St. Paul. Volume on the Midwest Exchange is only 2% or 3% of what it is on the Big Board.

Other regional exchanges include the Philadelphia-Baltimore Stock Exchange and those in Boston, Cincinnati, Detroit, Los Angeles, New Orleans, Pittsburgh, Salt Lake, San Francisco, Spokane, and Washington. All these exchanges are registered with the Securities & Exchange Commission, which means in effect that the Commission has approved their rules and regulations as being adequate for the discipline of any member who violates his public trust. The exchanges in Colorado Springs, Richmond, Wheeling, and Honolulu are exempt from regulation because they are so small.

The *regional exchanges* were organized originally to provide a market place for the stocks of local companies, but as these companies grew and acquired national reputations, many of them wanted their securities listed on an exchange in New York City, the nation's biggest money market. And so naturally did the Big Board. As it succeeded in luring many issues to New York, the regional exchanges languished.

But in recent years, the regional exchanges have managed in a small way to turn the tables on the Big Board. They have begun to trade in the same securities that are listed on the New York Stock Exchange, and today the business they do in these stocks is twice as big as the business done in their own listed local stocks. Furthermore, it's a business that is growing every day.

To get this business in Big Board stocks, the regional exchanges have induced some of the big companies to list their securities on one or more of the local exchanges as well as on the New York Stock Exchange, and if a company hasn't wanted to go to that expense, the regional exchanges have simply made their own arrangements to trade in those securities without formal listing. Such arrangements must be approved by the Securities & Exchange Commission.

At the end of 1951, almost 160 of the leading stocks — stocks that account for more than 40% of Big Board volume — were being traded on four or more regional exchanges, and in these stocks, the out-of-town exchanges now do about 10% as much business as the New York Stock Exchange. The Curb has not shared in this bonanza, because under SEC rules a stock cannot be listed on two exchanges in the same city.

When a Big Board stock is traded on a regional exchange, the price is generally determined by the last price shown on the New York Stock Exchange ticker. There is no auction, no bargaining to speak of. The specialist who handles such a stock simply bases his bid-and-offering quotations on the last ticker price, and he will buy or sell either round lots or odd lots. On odd lots, he will charge just what is charged on the Big Board, either ¼ or ⅛ point. Thus, the buyer pays just about what he would if his order were handled on the New York Stock Exchange. The seller gets a little extra break because he doesn't have to pay the New York state transfer taxes, although on exchanges in Massachusetts and Pennsylvania he will also encounter state taxes.

New York Stock Exchange member firms are most likely to execute orders for such stocks in the New York market even though they may also be members of a regional exchange where the stock can also be bought or sold. Of course, if such a broker gets an order for a Big Board stock after that exchange is closed for the day and if it can still be executed on some other exchange, such as San Francisco, which is still open because of the time difference, he can execute it there if the customer wishes. This situation sometimes permits a man to make an advantageous trade if a big piece of news breaks after the close of the New York market.

Local brokers and dealers are the ones who are profiting most handsomely from the availability of New York stocks on the regional exchanges, and nothing annoys the New York Stock Exchange more, because it feels that these local brokers are making a profit out of an auction operation to which they make no contribution. Local brokers retort that they are broadening the market and offering a tax saving on sales.

Actually, the Big Board hasn't been hurt in any significant way. Its percentage of the total listed securities business has scarcely changed a point in twenty years.

The most important new competition that faces the New York Stock Exchange today comes not from the regional exchanges in the United States, but from the exchanges north of the border, where the big postwar boom has stimulated world-wide interest in the ownership of Canadian stocks.

As a consequence, the volume of shares traded on the *Toronto Stock Exchange* in 1952 exceeded that of the New York Exchange by about one third, and seats on the Toronto Exchange have sold at prices that match those of the Big Board. However, a great deal of the Toronto trading is in the low-priced, highly speculative mining and oil shares — stocks that sell at an average price of only a little more than $2 a share, some for as little as two or three cents. So despite the great market activity, the actual dollar value of shares traded is less than 10% of the comparable figure for the New York Exchange.

The *Montreal Stock Exchange, Montreal Curb Exchange, Vancouver Stock Exchange,* and *Calgary Stock Exchange* now also rank among the first dozen exchanges on the North American continent. Interest in oil and mining shares runs especially high in Western Canada, while industrial shares are still the prime attraction on the more staid markets in Montreal, which used to dominate the Canadian securities scene until the boom gave Toronto its chance to take over the leadership. The Toronto Exchange boasts the most modern plant and the best mechanical facilities of any exchange in the world, facilities that have enabled it to handle a volume exceeding 12,000,000 shares a day without undue strain.

While many of the common stocks listed on the Toronto and Montreal exchanges are on a dividend-paying basis, the average return on them — about 4% or 5% — is a little lower than it is for those listed on the New York Stock Exchange and not nearly so many of them can boast of having paid continuous dividends over a long period of years.

But then the typical buyer of Canadian stocks — or "shares," as he usually calls them — isn't so interested in dividends anyway. He buys common stocks because he wants to share in the dynamic growth of the country and its industry, and he expects his shares to pay him a handsome profit over the years ahead.

If he really wants to invest his money for the sake of earning a prudent annual return, the Canadian is apt to think pretty exclusively in terms of bonds or preferred stocks.

In 1949, however, a change was made in the Canadian tax law which promises to effect an important change in this general attitude. The Canadian government now permits the taxpayer to reduce his income tax payment by an amount equal to 10% of whatever dividends he collects in a given year on common or preferred stocks issued by Canadian companies.

In the main, stocks are traded on the Canadian exchanges very much as they are in the United States, but there are several significant differences.

For one thing, floor trading is not restricted exclusively to member brokers. Thus, on the Toronto exchange every member is permitted to appoint as many as five "attorneys" to execute orders for him. Such attorneys must be approved by the Exchange as qualified for their jobs.

Again, there is no formal system of specialists who make markets in various stocks by buying or selling them for their own account such as there is on the New York Stock Exchange.

There are also significant differences in the units of trading. Thus, on the Toronto Exchange, oil and mining stocks selling at less than $1.00 a share — the so-called "penny stocks" — are traded in units of 500 shares, and if the price is $1.00 or more, the trading unit is 100 shares. On industrial stocks — principally the shares of manufacturing or distributing companies — still different units of trading are employed. On such stocks selling at less than $25 a share, the unit is 100 shares; between $25 and $100, it is 25 shares; and if the price is over $100, it is 10 shares. All of these different units are known as *board lots* rather than round lots.

Odd lots can also be bought or sold on Canadian exchanges, but they are not handled by special odd-lot brokers as they are on the New York Stock Exchange, and the price of an odd lot is not automatically determined by the price that prevails on the next board-lot trade. Each odd-lot order is the subject of separate bargaining between two or more brokers on the floor. In general, orders for 5, 10, or 20 shares of a stock are handled expeditiously, but the man who wants to buy some irregular number of shares — 3, 13, or 23 — may encounter some difficulty.

As a matter of general practice, the odd-lot buyer of industrial shares on the Toronto Exchange is apt to have to pay about ⅛ or ¼ more per share than he would on a board-lot order, while on oil or mining shares, the extra cost will vary from a few cents a share on stocks selling under $1 to as much as 10¢ or 15¢ on stocks selling over $1.

Canada does not have a national agency like our own S.E.C. to police and regulate the securities business, but every province has its own securities commission, and since the speculative boom got under way they have had their hands more than full. For several years, high-pressure operators headquartered in Canada, some of them from the States, were peddling questionable oil and mining stocks south of the border by mail and phone. There was no effective way that our own S.E.C. could put a stop to these solicitations, but by 1952 the Canadian authorities had been able to catch up with most of the worst offenders and bring the situation under control.

However, it is still a good idea to check carefully with some established broker before signing up for a block of stock in the Pipe Dream Gold Mine. Don't worry about missing the chance of a lifetime. If the stock is worth buying at all, it will probably be just as good a buy a couple of days from now as it is today.

Chapter 14
How the "Over-the-Counter" Market Works

IF you can buy the stocks and bonds of only about 4000 companies on the registered stock exchanges, where, you may ask, can you buy or sell the securities of the tens and tens of thousands of other companies that exist in this country? Suppose you wanted to buy or sell the stocks or bonds of these companies; how would you go about it?

Where, for instance, would you have bought the stock of the Rod & Reel Company in the days when it was growing up and before it ever could hope to be listed on any exchange?

The answer is that you would have bought it in the *over-the-counter* market, and that's where you buy or sell all the other *unlisted* securities today. Actually, this market isn't a place; it's a way of doing business, a way of buying and selling securities other than by the auction method that prevails on the exchanges.

When you deal in this market, you deal by private trade. You ask, "How much will I have to pay?" And the dealer asks in effect, "How much will you pay me?" He is not acting as your agent trying to buy or sell something for you at the best price possible; instead he bargains with you as one principal with another. He doesn't collect a commission; he tries to make a profit.

The term "over the counter" goes back to early Colonial times when the few securities that existed were often traded by a merchant, just like other merchandise, right over the counter in his store or office. It's an unfortunate label, because it suggests all the shenanigans that are associated with the phrase "under the counter," but it will not die, despite concerted efforts to substitute other terms, such as "unlisted" or "*off board*" or "*off exchange.*"

To illustrate how this market works, suppose that Rod & Reel common stock is not listed on any exchange and that you want to buy 50 shares of it. You go to a security dealer and place your order. Let's assume that he doesn't own any Rod & Reel himself and hence cannot sell the stock to you out of the inventory of stocks that he does carry. So he calls another dealer who does have some and asks the price. He may check two or three other dealers to see if he can get a better price.

Let's say the best price anyone quotes him is 18½ or $18.50 a share. That is the *inside price* to him, the price one dealer quotes another. It's not the price at which he'll sell to you. That price, the *outside price,* may be 19 or even more.

Whatever the price, it will be a *net price* to you — all you have to pay. You won't be charged a commission. The price is all-inclusive. Of course, instead of a commission, the dealer makes a profit. Often the profit is larger than the commission would be if you bought a stock selling at the same price on the New York Stock Exchange.

Thus, if the dealer charged 19, he would make ½ point on each share or $25 on the transaction, while the New York Stock Exchange commission on 50 shares of a stock selling at 18½ would be $14.25, plus the ⅛ point for the odd-lot broker, or $6.50, a total of $20.75, as compared with $25. But this, of course, is something the dealer isn't apt to tell you. Instead, he may even make a point of the fact that your purchase is "absolutely commission-free," as though he were giving you something for nothing.

If you are selling at net instead of buying at net, the dealer may follow much the same procedure. He will check other dealers and perhaps discover that the best price anyone will pay is 18¼. He might then offer to pay you 18 or 17⅞, and that again would be a net price. You wouldn't have to pay a commission. The dealer would absorb that, but you would have to pay transfer taxes.

Perhaps after he bought the stock from you, your dealer might decide not to sell it to the other dealer who had bid 18¼ for it. Perhaps he thinks he can make a bigger profit on it if he holds it himself. There may have been three or four other people who have come to him lately and expressed an interest in Rod & Reel Company. He might be able to sell it to one of them at 19 and make a much larger trading profit for himself. Or the stock might even go higher in a little while. He has looked into the Rod & Reel situation himself, and prospects appear good. Maybe the dividend will be increased. Maybe in a few months he will be able to sell the 50 shares at 20 or 21 or better.

For any or all of these reasons, the dealer might decide to

keep the stock himself. If he does, he is said to "*take a position*" in the stock. If he buys and sells it regularly himself, he is said to "*make a market*" in the stock, very much as a specialist does on the New York Stock Exchange.

Once a dealer makes a market in a stock, he is expected to be willing to buy it or sell it at any time and to announce the prices at which he is willing to trade it.

These prices will be of two kinds. There will be the inside or wholesale prices for other dealers — perhaps 18¼ bid, offered at 18½ — and the outside or *retail* prices for his customers, which might be 18 bid, offered at 19.

Price ranges such as these are the kind that might prevail on a stock that was fairly active. If the stock were inactive, there might be a considerably wider *spread,* on both the inside and outside markets, between what a dealer would be willing to pay for a stock and what he would ask for it if he were selling it.

Thus, if Rod & Reel were not well known, his risk in taking a position in that stock would be greater. He might have only occasional buying inquiries, and perhaps the only way he could ever move it would be to go out and sell it aggressively himself.

On a stock such as that, the dealer might have a spread of a full point or more between the inside buying and selling prices. As for the outside or retail prices, he'd be tempted to charge what the traffic would bear. He would buy it as cheap as he could and sell it as dear as he could.

Various factors determine just how much profit a dealer can expect to make on any stock. One of those factors is competition. If there are two or three other dealers in the same community making a market in the same popular, active stock, the prices of all of them are apt to be pretty much in line. At least the inside or dealer prices are, because they all know what each other will buy or sell the stock for.

As a matter of fact, any or all of them may publicly announce those prices in the *"pink sheets"* published daily by the *National Quotation Bureau,* a privately owned price-reporting service in the over-the-counter market. Every day the pink sheets report the inside prices on five or six thousand different unlisted stocks, as quoted by hundreds or thousands of different dealers.

Any dealer who wants to have his prices quoted supplies them every afternoon to the Bureau. The quotation sheets are mimeographed overnight and published the next morning in three different editions — Eastern, Western, and Pacific Coast. Since any dealer who has an important position in a stock wants to stimulate inquiries about it from other dealers, the pink sheets, subscribed to by almost every important dealer in the country, render a valuable service.

Quite obviously the pink sheets do much to stimulate competition and keep prices on the inside market pretty well regularized. Their influence on the outside or retail market is less direct, but standardized inside prices do make for more uniform profit margins on the part of the competitive dealers.

Another factor that will determine how much profit a dealer will expect to realize is the amount of effort he must expend in buying or selling a stock for you. Suppose you were in New York and wanted to dispose of some stock you owned in a little lumber company out in Oregon, a company that was virtually unknown outside its home town. Your dealer might not be able to get a bid from any other dealer in New York, where most of them are congregated. He might then try his luck in Chicago or San Francisco or Portland by calling or teletyping dealers in those cities. Ultimately, to promote a bid, preferably more than one, he might wire or phone local banks in the area to see if they knew of any possible buyers. He might even phone the company itself to see if it wanted to buy any of its own stock.

How much is all that effort worth?

Obviously there can be no pat answer to that. The nearest thing to a standard is the general agreement of dealers that the profit margin should not exceed 5%, unless special circumstances justify a greater change.

This was the standard arrived at by the Board of Governors of the *National Association of Security Dealers,* which represents about 3000 dealers in the country. The N.A.S.D. is much more than just a trade association; it is the official policeman of the over-the-counter business, designated as such by the Securities & Exchange Commission in 1938 and responsible to that agency. The N.A.S.D. has promulgated rules and regulations to assure fair practices, and it has reported a number of violations to the S.E.C. Up to 1953, 286 firms had been censured, fined, or suspended, and 81 had been expelled.

The N.A.S.D.'s regulating job is a tough one because of the sheer size and formlessness of the over-the-counter market.

The exact dimensions of the over-the-counter market are not known and probably never can be measured with any exactness, but it is generally assumed that the volume of business transacted in that market is probably greater than that of the New York Stock Exchange in an average year, and the number of individual stock and bond issues traded over the counter may be thirty or forty times as great.

Just the simple problem of defining what is meant by the over-the-counter market is itself difficult. For instance, the characteristic trade might involve the purchase of some unlisted security that enjoyed a regional rather than a national reputation — perhaps some stock like Rod & Reel; it would be bought from a local dealer, a man who was not affiliated with any member firm of the New York Stock Exchange; and the transaction would take place at a net price.

Now let's look at some aspects of the over-the-counter business which fail to square with this characteristic picture.

In the first place, not all of the securities sold over the counter are unlisted. Many stocks listed on the New York, Curb, and regional exchanges are frequently sold in private trades at a negotiated price instead of by auction on the exchange. The exchange market for some of these stocks is more fictional than real. Days and weeks may pass without a single trade in the security, and there may be a wide gap, maybe three or four points, between the bid-and-asked prices on such a stock.

In a case like that, the buyer or seller, particularly of a sizable block, can very often get a better price in a private trade than he can by exposing his bid or offer on the exchange. Even stocks listed on the New York Stock Exchange are not immune to competition from big over-the-counter dealers who will often offer a better price on a large block of some stock than the owner might be able to realize if he offered it on the Exchange floor and took the risk that the very size of the block might depress the stock's price under the Exchange's auction system.

In the second place, the characteristic picture is not wholly accurate because a big part of over-the-counter trading doesn't involve stocks at all. It involves bonds. Virtually all government bonds traded in the open market are sold over the counter either by banks or by a few large independent dealers. The New York Stock Exchange business in government bonds represents only a tiny fraction of 1% of the business handled over the counter. All municipal bonds and the great bulk of corporate bonds are similarly traded over the counter.

Thirdly, even as regards stocks, the typical picture has its shortcomings because not all over-the-counter stocks are those of little-known companies. Not by any manner of means. The stocks of Crowell-Collier Publishing Co., Weyerhaeuser Timber, and Time, Inc., for example, are sold only over the counter. So are many local utilities. And virtually all bank and insurance company stocks are sold over the counter in the United States rather than on exchanges as they are in Canada. Certainly nobody would describe the Chase National Bank or the Bank of America as little known. Many other over-the-counter stocks enjoy tremendous local prestige in various parts of the country — Bullock's on the Coast, Ralston-Purina around St. Louis, Plymouth Cordage in Boston, and Dan River Mills in the Carolinas, for instance.

As far as quality of stocks is concerned, the over-the-counter market runs the whole gamut of possibilities — from the rankest speculation, such as the penny oil and mining stocks, to others that cost thousands of dollars a share. In 1952, two of the highest-priced stocks were Los Angeles Turf Club at $47,500, and San Francisco Bank at about $20,000.

In the fourth place, the characteristic picture can be wrong because in buying an unlisted stock, you might find yourself dealing not with some little security dealer in Hay Center, Kansas, but with one of the biggest houses in Wall Street. Most of the big member firms of the New York Stock Exchange — the so-called wire houses — operate not only as brokers, executing Big Board orders for standard commissions, but also as dealers who buy and sell securities in private trades on a net-price basis. Usually, their over-the-counter business is handled by separate *trading departments,* but their salesmen solicit orders both for stock exchange and unlisted business.

The handling of transactions on a net-price basis rather than on a commission is the one characteristic of the picture which most nearly fits all over-the-counter trades. And yet there are even exceptions to this.

To avoid any possible charge of taking unfair advantage of a customer, some member firms of the New York Stock Exchange will handle even over-the-counter business on a regular commission basis. They do this by taking the best inside price they can get on any security that a customer may want to buy and adding to that figure the exact commission which they would receive on the same number of shares of a stock selling at the same price if the order were to be transacted on the New York Stock Exchange. A sell order would be handled at the same standard commission cost, plus transfer taxes.

However, not all the brokers and dealers who are willing to handle over-the-counter business on a commission basis are equally willing to adhere to the New York Stock Exchange commission schedule. They feel that they are entitled to ask higher commissions — sometimes appreciably higher — because of the greater risks they run in buying and selling securities for their own account.

When dealers buy or sell unlisted stocks, they do not make an odd-lot charge, because there are no round lots or odd lots in the over-the-counter business. A dealer will buy or sell any number you wish, but the profit margin he will try to make will naturally be proportionately greater on the smaller units.

What can the buyer or seller do to be sure that he's getting a fair price in an over-the-counter transaction?

One thing he might do is check the financial page of his local newspaper or some nearby metropolitan paper to see if it publishes bid-and-asked prices on the over-the-counter stock in which he is interested. These are furnished the press every day by the N.A.S.D. Some big-city papers publish such *quotations* on hundreds of over-the-counter securities regularly. Even some small-town papers publish prices on dozens of stocks in which there may be local interest.

None of these quotes is really an actual price. They are really only indications of the price range. Furthermore, it should be remembered that these are the outside or retail prices, and not infrequently the customer may do a little better than the published prices. Not anxious to embarrass its members, the N.A.S.D. is likely to quote prices that are a little padded. The padding isn't much in a bid quotation — what the dealer will pay for stock — but the asked price, if you want to buy, is apt to be quite inflated.

Again, to protect himself, the buyer can shop around and ask a couple of different dealers for a price on the same security. No dealer, of course, can guarantee the price he quotes a customer unless the order to buy or sell is placed right then. If the customer takes the time to check other dealers, he runs the risk of a disadvantageous price change, but the reassurance which he thus gains can make the risk well worth taking.

Finally, he can ask the dealer what the inside price is and whether he will handle the transaction on a commission basis instead of at a net price and what that commission will be.

This kind of query is certain not to improve the customer's popularity with those thousands of dealers whose whole business is done in the over-the-counter market. They strongly resent the competition of the New York Stock Exchange wire houses and the willingness of some of them to sell unlisted securities on a regular minimum commission basis.

They argue with considerable right on their side that they deserve to earn a larger profit on routine over-the-counter orders than their big competitors to whom the business may be only a sideline because of the special services that they as independent dealers render when new issues of stocks or bonds are floated.

After all, almost without exception these new issues make their debut in the over-the-counter market, and they might not be sold, the dealers contend, if it were not for them and their salesmen out pushing doorbells, wearing out shoe leather, and burning up gas — often for a return not sufficient to cover their expenses. Furthermore, new issues for existing companies could not be profitably sold if it were not for the fact that over-the-counter dealers are constantly risking their capital to make a market in those securities that the company has already issued.

And where, they ask, would the big New York underwriters be when it came to selling these new issues if the local dealers were unable to keep themselves alive by taking a 4% or 5% profit on an over-the-counter transaction instead of 1% or 2% commission?

Chapter 15
Investing — Or What's a Broker for?

SUPPOSE you decide that the time has come for you to put some of your extra savings into securities. What do you do next? How do you go about buying stocks or bonds?

You might go to your local banker and ask him how to proceed. He'll know several investment firms in your general community and probably at least one man in each of them. But don't forget that the banker is actually in competition with those security houses for your savings. He may buy government bonds or other securities from them himself, but the typical banker outside the big city banks is quite apt to look with a jaundiced eye on *your* buying securities. He'd rather see you add to your savings account or employ your money in other ways through his bank.

Again, don't forget most bankers are extremely conservative. It's their business to be. When it comes to investing the bank's own money, they have been legally compelled to confine those investments largely to government and other high-grade bonds. They have little familiarity with stocks and understandable misgivings about them — and that's often true even if they invest trust funds for customers. They don't realize that the individual's investment problem is apt to differ considerably from a bank's problem.

And what is true of a banker is apt to be true of a lawyer too. He's likely to be almost as conservative, because he thinks of investments principally in his role as a trustee, a man legally responsible for the administration of an estate.

So where else might you turn for help if you want to buy securities?

The answer to that is — a broker, because he's obviously the man best qualified to help you with your investment problem. That's his whole business. If you don't know the name of a broker, some one of your friends or associates surely does. And if you don't want to ask, look in the financial section of your daily newspaper. You'll find brokers' advertisements there. Study those advertisements for a while; find out which firm seems to have the kind of policies you like. Then go see them. You don't need a letter of introduction.

Lots of people still shy away from the broker for a variety of reasons. Some of them feel embarrassed about the amount of money they have to invest. Maybe they only have $500 to put into stocks, perhaps only $25 or $30 a month, and they figure a broker wouldn't be interested.

Maybe some brokers wouldn't be, but the big wire houses are spending hundreds of thousands of dollars in advertising every year to tell the smaller investor that they definitely are interested in him and in helping him invest his money wisely. So does the New York Stock Exchange.

And still people hesitate. Perhaps they think of the broker as a somewhat forbidding individual, who gives his time only to Very Important People, people who are well-heeled and travel in the right social circles. That's not true. There's nothing exclusive about the brokerage business today. No spats or striped pants. The club rules are all changed, and beer and hamburger are more popular items on the club menu than champagne and caviar.

Another thing that stops a lot of people is the jargon that brokers talk. You know now that there's nothing mysterious about words like debenture or cumulative preferred or stock dividend. True, they're specialized words because they apply to very specialized things, but there's nothing difficult to understand about either the words or the things they stand for, if you take the trouble to learn them (as indeed you are).

Finally, some people don't want to go to a broker because frankly they distrust him. They're afraid of being sold a bill of goods, a block of stock in some worthless company. That happened back in the twenties. Nobody can deny it. Maybe it happened to people you know — your father, your uncle, some member of your family.

Can it happen today? Yes, it *can* happen, but the important point is that it *doesn't* happen — not once in thousands and thousands of cases. A broker may try to sell you on the idea of buying stocks, because he believes in investing, but he hasn't any selfish reason to try to sell you any particular stock on the New York Stock Exchange, because his only return is the standard commission he earns on your order. As far as that commission is concerned, the difference between what he makes if you put a given amount of money into one stock rather than the same amount into another is usually so slight that it doesn't much matter to him which you buy.

Of course, when you buy stocks on a net basis — unlisted stocks — there is more of a chance that you can be sold something, something the dealer has an interest in unloading at a profit. But that doesn't happen very often. Few businesses are as competitive as the American securities business today, with every broker and dealer in the country anxious to get customers and keep them for a good many years to come. In that kind of situation there's not much room for the second-story operator who plays fast and loose with the customer's best interests. That character, the swindler of widows and orphans, is today a figment of the tabloid writer's imagination —or rather his lack of imagination.

Credit the Securities & Exchange Commission, if you please. Or credit the Stock Exchange's own housecleaning. Or credit the moral-making influence of a healthy competition.

But credit also the fact that the men in the securities business are in the vast majority of cases men of conscience and probity, responsive to a standard of ethics as high as prevails in any business you can name.

What it all comes down to is this: The safest way to begin investing is to buy some listed stock through a member firm of the New York Stock Exchange. The standard scale of commissions leaves no room for sharp practice.

If there's no member firm near you, you can write to one and buy by mail. Or you can order the stock through virtually any bank or security dealer in the country, although you may have to pay an additional charge. That charge is wholly legitimate.

But if the dealer you talk to tries to dissuade you from buying a listed stock, if he tries to switch you into Wildcat common or some other dubious stock, you had better check with another house. The dealer may have good reasons for believing that Wildcat common is a better security for you, and he might even be right. But there's also a chance that you've met up with the one character who can lend legitimacy to the tabloid writer's picture of the securities business.

Chapter 16
What It's Like to Do Business
with a Broker

LET'S assume you finally make up your mind to buy some stock like General Motors or General Electric and you go to a broker, a member firm of the New York Stock Exchange, to place your order.

What's likely to happen? What's a broker's office like? What do you say and what do you do? How does he operate?

A lot of people go in and out of a broker's office all the time, people who want to look at the ticker tape and see how some particular stock is doing. So if nobody pays any attention to you when you walk in, don't feel that you're being neglected. Just walk up to the first person who looks as though he works there and tell him you would like to talk to somebody about buying some stock. That will get action fast.

Maybe that person will take you to the manager who in turn will introduce you to a *registered representative* with whom you can discuss your problem in more detail. Maybe you'll skip the manager and be referred direct to some registered representative.

What's a registered representative? In the twenties he was called a *customer's man*. That's not a title in favor any more, because the customer's man got a bad reputation as a fast-work artist with a glib line when it came to selling bonds to old college chums or clubhouse cronies. Today's registered representative bears little resemblance to that character.

Again, the old customer's man used to "play the market" a good deal himself. Most brokers now are happy to see their employees invest in securities, but they frown on too much "in and out" trading by a registered representative for his own account. And they can keep close tab on that because of a New York Stock Exchange rule which forbids any employee of a brokerage firm to buy or sell securities except through the firm for which he works.

Many a customer refers to the registered representative as "my broker." Actually, of course, he isn't. He is an employee of the brokerage firm, and he simply represents the firm's broker who will execute your orders on the floor of the Exchange. That's why he's called a representative. The "registered" part of his title means that he has been approved by the Exchange as a man of good character and one who is thoroughly informed about the operations of the security business. In fact, he has had to pass a searching examination in the subject, administered by the Stock Exchange.

Registered representatives — also called *customer's brokers* or *account executives* by some firms — come in all kinds and qualities. Some are young, and some are old. Some are Democrats — yes, Democrats — and some are Republicans. Some have been in the business for years, and some are comparative newcomers.

These newcomers deserve a special word, because their entrance into the field is itself an evidence of how the business has changed. From the time of the depression to the end of World War II, only a handful of college graduates went into Wall Street. They looked for greener pastures — the big corporations.

But nowadays the securities business is getting its share of the topnotch men — and women too — from every graduating class. Many an old customer's man coasted for years on his reputation as an all-star halfback. His successor's career is apt to be based much more solidly on a record of real scholastic achievement, plus extracurricular leadership.

Again, the customer's man of yesteryear rarely bothered to acquire any formal training in the business; he just picked it up as he went along. The present-day registered representative has usually put in a much more painstaking apprenticeship. Often he has attended some firm's training school, plugging away eight hours a day for several months at basic lessons in finance, economics, and security analysis.

The registered representative is the man you deal with when you do business with a brokerage firm. He's usually assigned to you by the manager of the office, and if at any time you find his services less than satisfactory, all you have to do is ask the manager to be assigned to another man.

And if you don't like the brokerage firm itself, try another. There are hundreds of them, some big and some little, some competent and some not, some with special service and facilities and some with little more than a desk and a telephone.

Any of them can buy and sell securities for you, and all of

them will execute your orders faithfully; they won't bucket them. A *bucket-shop* operator is a man who accepts your order to buy a stock — and your money — but he doesn't execute the order; instead he pockets your money and gambles on his ability to buy the stock for you some time later at a lower price and make a profit for himself on your order. Needless to say, all such operations are thoroughly illegal, and today they are virtually nonexistent, thanks to the vigilance of the Securities & Exchange Commission and the Stock Exchange.

You can talk to your registered representative with complete candor, because whatever you tell him about your affairs will be held in strict confidence. A broker never reveals who his customers are, much less anything about their circumstances.

The more you tell him about your finances — your income, your expenses, your savings, your insurance, and whatever other obligations like mortgage payments you may have to meet — the better will he be able to help you map out an investment program suited to your needs.

It is part of his job to see that you get information or counsel whenever you need it. Don't be embarrassed about asking him the simplest kind of question about investing, about a company, about some financial term, or about the ticker and the *quote board* which are the focal point of interest in every brokerage office.

The tape offers a free show and a fascinating one. Some board watchers have been coming into the same broker's office, sitting in the same chair, every day for years, just for that show. Their number always increases when the weather is bad outside, and they constitute a real problem to the broker. They take up space for which he pays substantial rent; they contribute few commissions, and they often make it difficult for the cash customer to fight his way through to the desk of his own registered representative.

The tape itself is no longer what it was in the days when conquering Channel swimmers rode up Broadway through paper snowstorms. Except in rare cases, the ticker tape isn't even paper any more. It's made of cellophane, and it is projected on a ground-glass screen by a movie machine owned and operated by the Translux Movie Ticker Corporation. As the stock symbols and price figures march across this eight-foot screen, everybody in the board room can see as many as six or eight of the last reports on sales.

Many brokers have a *Translux,* as the ticker has come to be called, not only for New York Stock Exchange transactions but also for the Curb Exchange and for some commodity markets.

In addition to the ticker, all brokers also have a quote board or stock board, on which the prices are posted for a number of leading stocks, sometimes only a hundred stocks and sometimes as many as five hundred. For each of these stocks, the board usually shows the price of the stock at yesterday's close and today's opening of the market, the highest and lowest prices today, and the price on the last reported sale.

Many of these stock boards in the Northeast and on the Pacific Coast are electrically operated through a central service which is sold to brokers by the Teleregister Corporation, an affiliate of Western Union. Whenever there is a sale in any stock which is "boarded," the little figures automatically click over to show the latest price information for that stock. All fractional prices are quoted in eighths so that a price of 26 4 means $26\frac{4}{8}$ or $26\frac{1}{2}$.

In those sections of the country where the electric board service is not available or in those offices where the broker's business doesn't warrant the expense of such an elaborate installation, the old-fashioned chalk board continues in use. Employees known as board markers take sections of the tape as it comes from the ticker and post the latest prices, erasing earlier ones as necessary.

If you want to know the latest price and the day's range on a popular stock like U.S. Steel, all you have to do is phone your representative. He can look at the board and give you complete information. If the stock is one that isn't boarded, he can get the latest bid-and-asked quotations for you in a few minutes by phoning or wiring.

And if you want to have a pretty good idea of what you might have to pay for a stock before you buy, don't hesitate to ask for a quote. After all, in a typical year, brokers may ask the Quotation Bureau of the New York Stock Exchange alone for as many as 20,000,000 quotes.

One more call won't hurt.

Chapter 17
How to Open an Account

EVERY new customer of a brokerage firm must open an *account* with that firm before he can either buy or sell securities.

Opening a *cash account* with a brokerage firm is very much like opening a charge account at a department store. It simply involves establishing your credit so that the broker is sure you can pay for whatever securities you order.

This is important, because when you place a market order for a stock, neither you nor the broker can know to the exact penny just what you will have to pay. You may know that the last sale took place at $18\frac{1}{2}$ a share, but when your order is executed, even a few minutes later, the price may have gone up or down by an eighth of a point, a quarter of a point, maybe more. So when the purchase is made, the broker assumes the responsibility of paying for the stock and sends you a bill, a bill that you are supposed to pay in four days.

Naturally, the broker wants assurance from a new customer that such a bill will be paid, and that's why he'll ask for a credit reference, such as a bank. The other questions on the new account form that you must fill out are all routine — who you are, where you live, where you work, whether you are a citizen. In some states, married women are not permitted to open brokerage accounts except with their husband's consent.

If your first transaction with a brokerage firm involves the sale of some stock that you already own, instead of a purchase, you will still be asked to open an account, because the brokerage firm must still comply with the Stock Exchange rule which compels every broker "to learn the essential facts" about its customers as a protection against fraud or other illegal practices. For one thing, the routine of opening an account provides the broker with some assurance that the securities you offer for sale are really yours.

A bearer bond, for instance, can be sold by anybody who holds it, and it might easily be a stolen certificate. Even a registered bond or a stock with your own name on it presents a problem to the broker. It may be made out in the name of John Smith and John Smith may bring it to a broker to sell it, but if he hasn't done business there before, how's the broker to know that he really is the Smith named on the security?

Many husbands and wives prefer to open *joint accounts* with a broker, just as they may have joint checking accounts. In case one of them dies, the other can freely sell the securities without waiting for the courts to unsnarl the legal problems that are involved in settling any estate. Joint accounts are also used by individuals who are not related to each other but who have pooled their resources in a co-operative investment venture, often just for the sake of reducing commission costs on their trades.

People occasionally want to open accounts for their children, but as a general rule, brokers will refuse to do this because *minors* are not legally responsible for their acts. If brokerage transactions were carried on in the name of a minor, he could, when he became of age, repudiate them, and the broker would have no redress. Furthermore, company transfer agents are extremely reluctant to register any stock in a minor's name, if they know he is a minor.

Some parents set up trust funds and get a court order appointing them as trustees so they can legally buy or sell stock for their children. This is an expensive and cumbersome procedure, although it does permit wealthy people to realize important tax savings. In ordinary cases it is much simpler for the parents to buy stock in their own names and hold it for their children until they come of age.

If you want to open a *margin account* instead of a regular cash account, so that you can buy securities by paying only a portion of their purchase price, the broker will want to be even more certain about your financial solvency. After all, when you pay only part of the cost, the broker has to pay the balance, and that money may be on loan to you a long time.

Once you have opened an account — cash, joint, or margin — you can buy or sell whatever you want to simply by phoning your representative — or writing or wiring him. Probably better than 80% of a broker's business comes to him by phone.

If you live outside New York and give an order to a registered representative or a correspondent of some brokerage firm, that order is teletyped into the New York headquarters of the firm, phoned over to its booth on the Exchange floor, and promptly executed. Then the process is put in reverse. The floor broker gives his clerk in the booth a report on the order and the price at which it was executed. The clerk phones this information back to the headquarters office, where a report of the sale or purchase is put on the teletype wire and sent back to your representative.

The entire operation can literally be accomplished while you may still be on the phone talking to your representative about other matters. On a market order for immediate execution the round trip from California to the Exchange and back again has been made in less than one minute. Actually five or ten minutes is more like par for the course, and if the stock you are buying is an inactive one it may take a lot longer.

In any event, once your order is executed, your representative will be glad to report to you. Whether you get the information by phone or not, you'll know the next day just what price you got on the order because you will receive in the mail your broker's formal *confirmation* of the transaction.

If you have bought stock, this will be your bill. If you have sold stock, the confirmation will be a report on what you have realized, and the proceeds of that sale will automatically be credited to your account, unless you specifically ask that payment be made direct to you by check. Some brokers pay interest on cash funds that accumulate in a customer's account in excess of a given figure such as $500. This interest, perhaps 1% a year, becomes payable when that money is used to buy other securities at some later date.

Of course if you sell stock, you must see that the stocks are delivered to the broker. Since you have an account with him, he is likely to know what stocks you own, and he will sell any of them for you on instruction, even if he does not have the certificates actually in hand. But he expects you to deliver the certificates, properly endorsed, as soon as possible after a sale, because he in turn must make *delivery* within four days under the *settlement rules* of the New York Stock Exchange.

So they won't have to bother with delivery problems, many security owners find it advisable just to leave their stock certificates or bonds with their broker. They are right there then when the owner wants to sell. Such securities are carried in the customer's account just as cash might be, and every month he gets a statement showing just exactly what securities and what funds are credited to him.

On stocks that are left with him, the broker will collect all the dividends that are due and credit them as cash to the customer's account. Similarly on bonds he will clip the coupons and see that the interest payments go into the customer's account. Further, some brokers will mail to the customer the regular financial reports on those companies whose securities he owns as well as all proxies and official notices of meetings, dividends, stock rights, conversion privileges, and the like.

When a customer leaves his securities with his broker, the actual shares of stock are sometimes segregated and kept in his individual account, very much as they might be if he rented a safe deposit box. As a general rule, however, this kind of custodian service is available only to those who own large amounts of securities. In all other cases, if a customer leaves his securities with his broker, they are held in "*street name.*" This means that all the shares of a given security owned by all the broker's customers are lumped together and held in the broker's name; he keeps his own records of just what each individual customer owns. Thus, a broker might hold 100,000 shares of U.S. Steel for two or three thousand individual customers. The shares would all be made out in the broker's name, but he would send each customer a monthly statement showing just how many of those shares were his.

There is one big advantage to leaving your stocks with your broker in street name: If you want to sell any of them, all you have to do is phone him and give him instructions. You don't even have to bother with endorsing the certificates.

But is it safe to leave your securities with your broker, as you might leave cash with your banker?

The answer to that is that it's probably safer to leave them with a broker than it is to try to take care of them yourself. They are stored in his vault, and he carries insurance on them. When they are left with him, they can't be lost or misplaced, and the risk of loss by fire or theft is probably much less than it would be if you kept them in your own home or office.

Furthermore, the broker cannot borrow money on those securities nor can he sell or lend any of them except on express authorization. Those securities belong to his customers. He is only the custodian. The surprise audits which are sprung on all member firms once a year by the New York Stock Exchange make sure that the broker is faithful to his trust.

But what if a broker goes under, despite all the regulations of the Stock Exchange and the Securities & Exchange Commission?

One answer to that is that they don't. Not as often as banks.

Despite 1929, brokers boast of a 99.77% *solvency record* over a fifty-year period. In that same period, state and national banks can show a solvency record of only 98.49%.

Furthermore, even if a brokerage firm did go bankrupt, a customer's stocks on deposit with a broker would not be involved, since these are not part of a broker's assets. He simply holds them as a custodian. If necessary, the customer could bring a recovery action against the partners of the brokerage firm, each of whom is individually liable.

Virtually all member firms of the New York Stock Exchange are *partnerships*. As a matter of fact, under the rules of the Exchange they had to be partnerships until May 1, 1953, when the regulation was amended to permit firms to incorporate if they wished to. This amendment meant that the large nonmember dealers, operating as corporations rather than partnerships, could buy Exchange seats if they wanted to.

Chapter 18
What It Means to Speculate

SPECULATING is an inevitable part of the business of buying securities. But then speculating is an inevitable part of just living.

Whenever you are confronted with an unavoidable risk — as indeed you are in many of your actions every day — you must speculate. You must meet the risk; you must take your chances. Often you are presented with a choice of risks; when you make up your mind about which one you will take, weighing the good and the bad features of each, you arrive at a speculative decision.

The Chicago businessman who must be in New York within twenty-four hours can fly or go by rail. He can figure on getting there faster if he flies, but there's always the possibility of bad weather, mechanical failure, even disaster. Those hazards may be somewhat reduced if he takes the train, but on the other hand, family or business circumstances may be such that it is desirable for him to make the trip in the shortest possible time. Faced with that kind of choice, the man must inevitably speculate.

The retailer who decides to stock up on a lot of goods is speculating on a price rise. He figures he can buy those goods cheaper now than he can some months later.

The manufacturer who must pick Jones or Smith for a key job must speculate on which will be the more able man.

And the farmer's whole operation is one vast speculation. When he puts the seed in the ground, he is speculating on his ability to grow a crop and sell it at a profit, despite weather, pests, blight, and changing market prices.

When a man takes a risk he cannot avoid, he is speculating. But when he takes a risk that he doesn't have to take, he gambles.

That is one distinction between speculation and gambling, and there is another. Speculation involves an exercise of reason, while gambling involves nothing but chance. The man who speculates can make an intelligent forecast of the hazards of his course. The gambler stands or falls on the flip of a coin or the draw of a card.

In the purchase of any stock or bond, even a government bond, there is an element of speculation, because the risk that it might decline in value cannot be avoided. For that matter, there is a risk in just having money — the risk that it won't buy as much when you want to spend it as it will today.

But when a man buys securities, he doesn't have to operate on the basis of chance. He can make a fairly intelligent estimate of just how much risk he assumes on the basis of the record. And he has a wide range to choose from — all the way from a government bond to the penny stocks of those companies whose assets may be made up principally of hope.

The word *investments* is technically applied only to government bonds, municipal bonds, and first-quality corporate bonds. To the conservative buyer of securities for a bank or an insurance company, all stocks are considered too risky to be classed as investments, despite the fact that some stocks have proved safer than lots of corporate bonds, particularly the debentures and secondary bonds of weak companies.

But because most preferred stocks and a good number of common stocks have shown themselves to be so stable, even the conservatives refer to them nowadays as "investment-type" securities. These are apt to be the stocks of utilities or food firms or banks or chain stores — industries that have shown themselves to be comparatively steady earners, come boom or depression.

Of course, what is one man's speculation is very often another man's investment, and below the level of top-flight securities is a vast assortment of stocks which many men of sound judgment consider good investments primarily because of the liberal dividends they pay — 6%, 8%, even 10% or more.

Often these are the stocks of companies whose fortunes rise and fall more sharply with the business cycle — companies in the automobile, steel, construction, or clothing industries. When business is good they pay excellent dividends, and when it slumps those dividends may be reduced or eliminated.

As a rough rule of thumb, the degree of risk which you assume in buying one of those middle-quality *"cyclical" stocks* can be measured by the liberality of the dividend. The larger the dividend as a proportion of the selling price, the greater the risk.

Then there are other stocks — thousands and thousands of them — that must be frankly classified as speculations. But even here there is a wide range of quality. At the top of the list are those stocks that might be described as "good *growth* situations." They are the stocks of companies, often paying little or no dividends, which are regarded as attractive because of future prospects. Thirty years or so ago, many of the automobile and radio stocks might have been so classified. More recently aviation, chemical, natural gas, air conditioning, and pharmaceutical stocks have often been placed in this category.

Some speculative securities are attractive not because the future is so glowing but simply because it looks a lot better than the past. A company may have had to pass some dividends or interest payments during a difficult period of reorganization, but once it starts to hit the come-back trail its securities are apt to take on new life. Many a sizable fortune has been made out of buying bonds that were severely depressed in price because the company had to default on bond interest payments for a period. And that's also true of many preferred-stock issues on which dividend payments have accumulated for a number of years and ultimately been paid off. But these are strictly long shots and must be so regarded.

Finally, there are the penny stocks. A few of these may be the listed securities of old-line companies that have fallen on evil days. Bankruptcy stares them in the face, and their stock seems virtually worthless. But by all odds the great majority of these low-priced stocks, selling at 50¢, $1, $2, maybe as high as $5, are issued by new ventures. They are not seasoned securities listed on the Big Board but rather they are stocks in questionable Canadian oil or mining companies that are peddled by high-pressure salesmen who expect to make as much as 50¢ on every dollar's worth they sell. Often by direct mail or even long-distance phone, the prospect is told that a block of 100 or 300 shares has been reserved in his name, but he must buy them within 48 hours or lose this chance of a lifetime. People who have charge accounts at expensive stores and professional people, such as doctors and lawyers, are particular targets for this kind of promotion, because their names and addresses are so easily available from direct-mail firms.

The most devastating thing is that these glamorous sales stories often have an element of truth about them. The men who put their money in the oil property "right next to our land" may actually have made 1000% on their investment already, but the fact remains that anyone who takes a flyer on this kind of a deal is much more apt to lose everything he puts into it than he is to make a whopping profit.

Although there is an obvious difference between this kind of rank speculation and the solid investment which a government bond represents, it is also true that the distinctions between investing and speculating frequently get hazy as soon as you move away from either of these two extremes. Actually, the difference between investing and speculating is not to be measured so much in terms of the individual security as it is in terms of the motive of the buyer.

The investor is a man who puts his money to work in a company in the expectation of earning a reasonable and regular return on it over the long pull. The speculator takes a short-term view. He is not interested in dividends; he is interested in making a quick profit on his money and selling out while he can get it. Often he takes a big risk in the process, but if he hits it right, he stands to make a lot of money.

Furthermore, under present federal tax laws he will probably be able to keep more of that money than he would if he made the same amount of money in dividends, salary, or other income.

Risk capital — the money that a man puts at risk when he buys or sells almost any kind of property — has played such an important role in building this country that Congress for more than a quarter of a century has always given favored tax treatment to profits realized in such ventures. These are called *capital gains,* and they include the profits realized on the purchase and sale of securities.

Tax rates change from year to year, but in 1952 the law provided that a man who made a capital gain on any security that he owned for more than six months — a *long-term* capital gain — would not have to pay a tax of more than 26% on that profit, and it might be considerably less, for instead of paying 26% on the entire gain, he could, if he chose, pay a straight income tax on only half the gain at whatever regular income tax rate applied in his case. On the other hand, *short-term* capital gains — those running for less than six months — were taxed at full regular income tax rates.

Wealthy men are apt to find stock speculation particularly attractive, because they have to pay taxes in high-income brackets, ranging up to 92%, and the favored tax treatment accorded long-term capital gains appeals to them.

Furthermore, the law offers them other special advantages. If a speculator has a capital gain of $5000 and a capital loss of $4000, he pays the gains tax on only $1000. If his losses exceed his gains, he can carry the losses over for several years and use them to reduce whatever tax he might have to pay on future capital gains. Finally, he is even permitted to deduct a maximum of $1000 a year of whatever losses he may suffer from his other income and thus reduce his regular tax.

Favorable as this treatment may appear to be, many economists argue that it is not favorable enough. They contend that new venture capital — speculative capital — should be made much more freely available to business and that this could be accomplished by reducing or eliminating the tax on long-term capital gains and by permitting the taxpayer to classify his profit as a long-term gain after a period of, say, three months instead of six. Canada has no capital gains tax, and that is one reason, they say, why Canadian business was able to attract twenty billions of new capital in the half-dozen years after the war.

(Regardless of what's good or bad about the capital gains tax, there is no question of the fact that our tax laws do discriminate against stock owners, speculators and investors alike, in one vital way: All stock dividends are subjected to *double taxation*. First, the company must pay a tax on its net earnings before dividends are paid, and that tax might typically cut the amount available for dividends by more than half. Then when the stockholder gets his dividends, he must report them as income and pay a regular income tax on them.)

Curiously enough, the professional speculator does not so often try to make a profit — a capital gain — by putting his money into a really speculative stock as he does by speculating in the fifty or sixty active stocks — many of them top-flight investments — that usually account for most of the transactions on the Big Board.

There is a reason for this. At any given time, the price of a stock or the price of all stocks represents the combined judgments of all the people who are buying and selling. Most times a speculator is staking his judgment against the public judgment.

He may study the stock of a company in minute detail, and on the basis of that intensive analysis, he may feel that he knows better than the public what it's really worth — or rather what the public will sooner or later take as its real worth.

Again, he may think that he has a better feel of the market as a whole, knows better than the public does whether stock prices generally will advance steadily upward in what is called a *bull market* or decline for a period of time in a *bear market*. If he is right, the leading stocks — those that enjoy the widest public following — will probably provide the earliest confirmation of his judgment and the most emphatic one.

On the assumption that his judgment is right, the speculator seeks to augment his profits — or protect them once they are made — by using various techniques of trading.

He may buy on margin.

He may pyramid profits.

He may sell short.

He may buy puts or calls.

And, as we shall see, none of these techniques constitutes in itself unfair or dishonest manipulation of the market.

Chapter 19
How Stocks Are Bought on Margin

ONCE a security buyer has assured a broker of his financial responsibility and opened a margin account, he can buy stocks just by making a down payment on them. How big that down payment must be is governed by various rules.

First, the New York Stock Exchange says that no one can buy its securities on margin unless the down payment is at least $500.

Then there are the special requirements set by individual brokers; some, for instance, will not permit a customer to buy any stock on margin unless it sells above $2 or $3 a share.

Finally and most important of all, there is the regulation exercised by the Federal Reserve Board which has been empowered by Congress to say, in effect, just what the minimum *margin requirements* must be. Since 1934, when the Board began to exercise its authority, it has set that minimum by saying that the down payment must represent a certain percentage of the total value of the stock that is being bought on margin. The percentage is changed from time to time, depending on how worried the Board is about inflation and about the amount of stock trading that is done on margin.

The lowest figure which the Board has ever set is 40%, and that figure prevailed for eight years from 1937 to 1945. The highest figure has been 100%, and while that was in effect from January, 1946, to February, 1947, nobody could buy on margin, for the minimum down payment required by the Board was equal to the full purchase price. In recent years, the figures of 50% or 75% have been most common.

Suppose the requirement at a given time is 50%. This means that you can buy $10,000 worth of some listed stock with $5,000 (unlisted stocks are not sold on margin), and the broker lends you the other $5000. Naturally when he does that, he charges you interest on the money he lends. How much interest depends on how much he in turn would have to pay a bank if he had to borrow the $5000 there, as he often does, to lend it to you. He'll charge you that interest plus, according to Stock Exchange regulations, at least ½ of 1% for himself. The total charge the broker makes may run anywhere from 3% to 4½%, and to many a broker the interest he earns on *margin loans* constitutes an important source of revenue.

When a broker borrows money at the bank to lend you so that you can buy stocks on margin, he has to give the bank some security on the loan. That security may be the very stock that you buy on margin. Hence, when you open a margin account, you must agree to leave your margined stocks with the broker and to let him *hypothecate* them or pledge them as security for whatever bank loan he may need in order to carry your margin account or those of his other customers.

If you were to buy $10,000 worth of stock on margin, you would naturally pay all commissions and taxes on the full $10,000 worth of stock. But you would also be entitled to receive all the dividends on those shares, and this alone is sufficient to interest many a man in buying stocks on margin, especially at a time when they are paying liberal dividends.

For instance, when stocks are paying 6% and 7% dividends, as they have been doing in recent years, the stock buyer stands to make a little extra profit just on his dividends if he buys on margin. Thus, by putting up only $5000 he might earn 6.5% on $10,000, or $650, while his costs would amount to only about $290 — $200 on a $5000 loan at 4% plus a $45 commission to buy the stock and another $45 to sell it. If he sold the stock at the same price that he paid for it, having neither a gain nor a loss there, he would have made a net profit, exclusive of transfer taxes, of $360.

In contrast, if he had used his $5000 to buy the stock outright, he would have had only half as many shares and received only half as much in dividends or $325. Meanwhile, his commission costs on buying and selling would have amounted to $80, leaving him a net profit, exclusive of taxes, of only $245. In other words, on the same amount of capital he could have made an extra $115 or about 44% more in dividends by buying on margin.

Comparatively few people use their margin accounts this way, partly because they don't understand the technique and partly because it won't work as successfully on small purchases. The higher commission rates on these purchases — not to mention the odd-lot charge of an extra ⅛ or ¼ share — can eat up the extra dividend profit which the margin buyer hopes to realize. So he must carry the extra risk involved in owning twice as many shares without any hope of a compensating increase in the dividend return.

More importantly, anyone who has the sizable funds which this kind of operation requires isn't interested in buying on margin for the sake of the little extra money he might earn in dividends. Nine times out of ten he's interested in margin for the sake of the extra speculative profit he hopes to make.

Margin is the speculator's Number 1 tool.

Suppose a man has picked out a stock selling at $50 a share which he thinks is sure to go up. Under a 50% margin rule, he can buy 200 shares of that stock instead of just 100 shares with his $5000. If it goes up five points, he makes $1000 instead of just $500, a 20% profit instead of 10%. That kind of profit can make the 4% interest which he may pay on his loan look cheap.

But suppose the stock goes down in price? There's the rub.

It's then that his broker may *call* on him to put up more margin — that is, to increase his down payment. If he can't put up more money, the broker has the right to sell his stock — as much of it as may be necessary — to raise the required cash. This presents no problem to the broker because all margined stocks must be left on deposit with him.

How much more money might a margin buyer have to put up if his stocks decline? The answer to this is governed by the *margin maintenance* rules of the New York Stock Exchange and those of the individual broker. The Federal Reserve Board isn't in the picture at all after the original purchase; if a buyer meets its margin requirements then — say, of 50% cash — he is never compelled by the Board to put up more margin, even if the Board raises its requirements to 75% or more.

Under the New York Stock Exchange rule, however, a broker must call on a customer for more margin whenever the amount that the customer would have left if he sold his stocks and paid off the broker's loan represents less than 25% of the current value of the stocks.

To illustrate: Suppose a man bought 100 shares of a stock selling at $30 a share at a time when the Federal Reserve Board required only 50% margin. In that case he would put up $1500, and he would borrow $1500 from his broker. Now suppose the stock dropped from $30 to $20 a share. If he were to sell out now, he would realize only $2000 on his holdings, and after he paid his broker $1500, he would have only $500 left, which would be exactly 25% of the current value ($2000) of his stock.

If the stock were to fall below 20 in this instance, the broker would have to ask for enough more margin money so that the 25% ratio would be restored. Actually, he'd probably ask for a little bit more so that he wouldn't have to make another margin call so soon again in case the stock continued to decline.

On a 50% margin basis, it is evident that a stock can drop a full third in price — from 30 to 20 — before a broker must call for more margin.

If the Federal Reserve Board's margin requirement was 75% instead of 50%, the stock could decline two thirds in value before the customer would have to put up more money. Here's how that works: the customer buys 100 shares of stock at 30 and puts up 75% margin or $2250. He borrows only $750 from the broker. If the stock drops to $10 his holdings are worth $1000. At that point, he could sell out, pay the broker $750, and still have $250 left, which would represent 25% of the current market value of his stocks ($1000).

The Federal Reserve requirement governing the initial margin payment and the Stock Exchange rule on maintenance of margin explain why margin calls are comparatively infrequent today.

Not only have the regulations resulted in a lot fewer margin calls than there were in the days after the 1929 crash but they have also greatly reduced the number of margin accounts. In 1929 it is estimated that there were 600,000 margin customers. They represented 40% of all customers, but they accounted for a considerably larger proportion of a broker's total business. Just how large a proportion no one knows exactly, but as the market boiled upward in the late twenties, the margin customers were always the big buyers, the people who kept *pyramiding* their *paper profits* and buying more and more stock.

Here's how pyramiding worked in those days. Suppose a man bought 200 shares of a $50 stock. Under the lax margin regulations which prevailed then he might have had to put up only $2000 of the $10,000 cost — maybe even less if he were a favored customer.

Now let's assume that his stock advanced to $75 a share. His total holdings would now be worth $15,000. If he were to sell at that price and settle the $8000 account with his broker, he would have $7000 cash; and on a 20% margin basis, this would enable him to buy $35,000 worth of stock. Actually, of course, he rarely had to go through the mechanics of selling out and buying afresh. The broker recognized the expanded value of his original holdings and accepted that added value as collateral on the additional purchases.

In this instance, the customer would have been able to own $35,000 worth of securities on a cash margin of only $2000, thanks to that 25% increase in the value of his original 200 shares. If he continued to be that lucky, he could run his paper profits to a hundred thousand dollars, a half-million dollars, a million dollars, many millions of dollars, all on just $2000 cash.

And in the twenties many people did exactly that. But when prices started to decline and the margin calls came, many of them couldn't raise even a few thousand dollars cash, except by selling securities. And when they sold, that very act of selling depressed prices further and resulted in more margin calls. Again they had to sell. And so the vicious circle kept swirling downward into the great abyss.

There's nothing illegal about pyramiding — even today under the Federal Reserve Board rules brokers can accept securities as well as cash on the required margin payment — but it just can't work very effectively when you have to put up margin of 50% or 75%, instead of 20%. Only a substantial increase in the price of your stock will yield you big enough paper profits to permit a significant increase in your holdings.

And that's another reason why margin accounts aren't as popular as they used to be. By the end of the war, they had declined to less than 10% of their number in 1929. In recent years there has been some increase, but margin buyers still represent only 10% or 15% of all the people who buy listed securities on the New York Stock Exchange.

So few is their number and so well protected are their margin accounts that even if there were a serious decline in the market, it is unlikely that it could ever be turned into the kind of rout that made 1929 the debacle it was.

Chapter 20
What It Means to Sell Short

WHEN a man opens a margin account with a broker, he is asked to sign an agreement giving the broker authority to lend his margined stocks to others. It is this lending agreement which makes it possible in most cases for other customers to sell stocks short.

Short selling accounts for only 3% or 4% of all the transactions on the New York Stock Exchange, and yet probably no other market technique excites so much public interest — or is so widely misunderstood.

A short sale is nothing but the reverse of the usual market transaction. Instead of buying a stock and then selling it, the "short" trader sells it first and then buys it back at what he hopes is a lower price.

If it is legitimate to buy a stock because you think it's going to go up, why isn't it just as legitimate to sell it because you think it's going to go down? Why shouldn't you be able to try to make a profit in either direction? It can be fairly argued that the right of a bear to sell *short* is just as vital to a completely free market as the right of a bull to buy stocks or go *long*.

Regardless of the logic of the situation, most people think it just isn't morally right to sell something you don't have.

What about the magazine publisher who sells you a three-year advance subscription to his publication?

Or what about the farmer who may sell his whole crop to a grain elevator or to a miller when the seed hasn't even sprouted yet?

Both of them sell something they haven't yet got just on the strength of a promise to deliver. And that's all a "short" seller does.

Furthermore, it isn't really true that he sells something he doesn't have. He has to *borrow* the stock that he sells, and he has to give it back. This he hopes to be able to do by *covering* or buying it back at a price less than he sold it for.

Where does he borrow his stock? From his broker.

Where does the broker get the stock to lend? Usually from his margin customers who signed the lending agreement when they opened their accounts. If a broker doesn't have among his margin accounts the particular stock that a man wants to sell short, he will borrow it from another broker or from some individual stock owner who makes a business of lending his stock. But the broker cannot borrow stock from the account of any of his cash customers without specific authorization.

Why should one broker lend stock to another? Because he gets paid for it — an amount equal to the value of the borrowed stock — and he has free use of this cash until the stock is returned. Sometimes if the stock is in demand, the borrowing broker will even pay a premium for the loan of it. Any such premium payment is, of course, charged to the "short" seller. If the value of a stock on loan increases significantly, the lending broker will expect more money; if it drops, the borrowing broker will expect a proportionate refund.

A "short" seller operates under essentially the same rules that govern margin buying. If the Federal Reserve Board has a 50% margin rule in effect, the seller must put up cash equal to 50% of the market value of the stock that he borrows and sells. Under Stock Exchange rules, the minimum margin cannot be less than $500; furthermore there can be no short sales on stocks selling for less than $5.

Suppose a man wanted to go short 100 shares of a stock selling at 30. If the Federal Reserve Board requirement was 50% at the time, he would have to put up $1500 cash. If the stock dropped to 25, he could buy it back, cover his short position by returning the stock, and make a profit of $5 a share or $500, less taxes and commissions.

But perhaps when the stock hits 25, he thinks it will go lower. He could make more money if it does, but he doesn't want to lose the profit he already has. In such a situation he might place a *stop order to buy* at 26. This is the exact counterpart of a stop-loss order that a man who owns stocks may use to protect himself when he's afraid the market will drop.* In this case, the "short" wants to protect himself against a rising market. If the stock does go up to 26, his stop order becomes a market order to buy at once.

If he buys back in at that price, he will still have a profit of $400, exclusive of all brokerage commissions and taxes. Additionally, he will also be liable for whatever dividends may have accrued on the stock during the operation, because the

* See p. 71.

lender obviously was entitled to get them during the time his stock was on loan.

This is one big reason why the "short" seller under the Stock Exchange rules has to maintain a margin of 30%, while the margin buyer is only required to meet a 25% figure.

The 30% margin requirement means that the broker will call for more money whenever the amount of margin that the "short" seller would have left if he bought the stock back and covered his short position would amount to only 30% of its current market price.

Suppose a man sells short 100 shares of a stock at 30. If the initial margin requirement were 50%, he would have to put up $1500. Now instead of declining to 25, suppose the price of the stock goes up to 35. If he were to cover at that point, he would have to pay out $3500 or $500 more than he sold the stock for originally. That means he would have only $1000 margin left in his account or just about 30% of the current value of the stock ($3500 × .30 equals $1050). At that point, unless he decided to take his loss and close out the transaction, he would get a call for more margin.

While it can be argued on the one hand that there is a legitimate place for short selling in a free and orderly securities market, it cannot be denied on the other hand that short selling has often been used for illegitimate purposes. From the time 350 years ago when buyers and sellers first began to trade in the stock of the Dutch East India Company, the history of short selling has not been a pretty one. But it has contributed some gaudy chapters to the history of the New York Stock Exchange, particularly in the nineteenth century when short selling was a favorite tool of such famous market manipulators as Commodore Vanderbilt, Daniel Drew, Jay Gould, and Jim Fisk.

In many battles, these men tried to catch each other in market corners. A market *corner* is created when one man or group succeeds in getting such complete control of a particular stock that others who may have sold it short cannot cover their purchases by buying the stock back, as they have to do, except on terms dictated by the controlling group.

One of the most classic corners is that which involved the old Harlem Railroad, a predecessor of the New York Central. Vanderbilt got control of the Harlem and then proceeded to extend the road down Manhattan Island. Drew, who was also a stockholder in the road and had realized a handsome profit as the stock advanced in price, now saw an opportunity to make a much larger profit. He induced the New York City Council to repeal the franchise which had been granted for the extension of the road. Simultaneously, he sold the stock short.

His maneuver did succeed in driving the price of the stock down, but as Drew sold, the Commodore bought. In the end, Drew and some of the members of the Council who were associated with him in this notorious exploit found that they had sold short more stock than actually existed. They could not cover their short positions except on terms dictated by Vanderbilt — and the terms were ruinous.

Even when nothing so titanic as an attempted corner was involved, short selling proved an effective manipulative device for *pool* operators who would join forces to bid the price of a stock up and then sell it short in order to make a big speculative profit.

Often such pool operators would risk very little of their own capital in the operation. They would stimulate public interest in a particular stock by adroit publicity and by creating considerable activity in the market for that stock. That activity was usually more apparent than real, because it would be generated by *wash sales*. A wash sale, now outlawed by the S.E.C., simply involved the simultaneous purchase and sale of large blocks, say 1000 or 10,000 shares. Such big volume would attract the public, which inevitably seems to buy whenever there is a lot of activity in a stock. As the public bought and as the price rose, pool operators would wait for the strategic moment when they thought the stock was about as high as it could get, and then they would begin selling it short, hammering the price down to a level where they could buy it back at a handsome profit.

One of the most important reforms introduced by the Securities & Exchange Commission is the regulation which now effectively prevents this abuse of the right to sell short. The S.E.C. accomplished this objective by a simple regulation which in effect provides that a stock can be sold short only on a rising market.

Technically the regulation, now rigorously enforced not only by the S.E.C. but by all stock exchanges, works this way: If a customer places an order to sell short, that order as it goes to the floor must be clearly marked as a short sale, and the floor broker is forbidden to execute that order except at what is, in effect, a higher price. Thus, if a stock were last sold at 50, the broker could not sell that stock short except at a price of 50⅛ or higher; in this case he would be selling on what is called an *up tick*.

There is one exception to this: The broker may sell the stock at 50, the same price as prevailed on the last sale, provided the last previous change in the price was upward. In other words, there might have been one or two or six transactions that had taken place at that same price of 50, but a short sale could still be made at 50, provided the last different price was 49⅞ or lower. This is called selling on an *even tick*.

Another S.E.C. rule which has proved helpful is one that prohibits officers and directors or others who are in a position to know the intimate affairs of a company from selling the stock of that company short. As a matter of fact, such officials are prevented from taking any short-term speculative profit in their company's stock. If an officer buys his company's stock, he can't sell it for the sake of taking a profit in any period less than six months. If he does, the management of the company or any individual stockholder can bring suit against him.

In the old days the directors of a company were occasionally guilty of trying to capitalize on their special knowledge. Thus, after a directors' meeting where it might have been decided to pass a dividend, some of the directors might rush to the phone to sell the stock short before the public ever got the news. The S.E.C. rules now prohibit these abuses.

These regulations explain why the volume of short selling has dwindled so. Nevertheless, on some of the leading stocks which may on occasion have been bid up to too high a price, short sales can account for a substantial proportion of all transactions — perhaps as much as 20% or 30% on a given day. But this is comparatively rare.

Most of the short selling which is done nowadays comes not from the public but from members of the Exchange. Does this mean that brokers are still up to their old manipulative tricks? Not at all.

Probably most of the short sales are made by the specialists, and they very often have to make these sales if they are to fulfill their obligations to conduct fair and orderly markets in the stocks they handle. Thus, if a broker wants to execute a market order for a customer and there are no other offers to sell, except perhaps at a price that is wholly out of line — perhaps as much as a full point higher — the specialist is expected to sell the stock at a better price, even if he doesn't have it in his inventory and has to go short in order to complete the transaction.

No short sales for their own account can be made by brokers who represent brokerage firms that do business with the public, but the floor traders and the $2 brokers can sell short. When they do, it is not because they are trading on inside knowledge; usually it's just because they are cynical about the public's perpetual bullishness.

The public always wants the market to go up. The public always thinks it will — and so buyers act accordingly. In this kind of situation, who would deny an old bear the right to bet that the bulls are wrong again?

Chapter 21
Puts and Calls, Plain and Fancy

IN addition to margin buying, pyramiding, and short selling, the speculator can execute still one other market maneuver which is especially useful if he wants to protect a profit he has already made or insure himself against loss. He can buy a *put* or a *call* on any listed stock through any one of about two dozen dealers who specialize in this business.

If he buys a put, he buys the right to sell 100 shares of a particular stock — if he wants to — within a given period of time at a specific price which is fixed in the contract.

A call is the exact opposite. The speculator pays for the right to buy 100 shares of a certain stock at a set price within a given period of time.

Both puts and calls are called *options,* since the buyer has the option of deciding whether he will exercise a put or a call after he has bought it. If he buys a call on a stock, he doesn't have to exercise it, doesn't have to buy the stock, but if the price of the stock goes up appreciably any time within the contract period, he can obviously realize a nice profit by calling on the dealer to sell him the stock at the guaranteed lower price. If he buys a call and the stock goes down, he loses whatever he had to pay for the call, because there would then be no advantage in exercising it.

The prices and terms at which put-and-call dealers will sell options are pretty well standardized. Thus there are two generally recognized types of options — the 30-day contract and those for longer periods — 60 days, 90 days, or six months.

On a 30-day call, the price that is set in the contract is usually a point or two above the current market price, and on a 30-day put it is a point or two below the present market. Thus, on a stock selling at 40, a price of 41½ might be set on a 30-day call and 38½ on a 30-day put. Such options usually sell at a cost to the buyer of $137.50, which on the basis of 100 shares figures out to 1⅜ points. Consequently, if you were to buy a call on this stock, it would have to go up to more than 42⅞ (41½ plus 1⅜) before you could show a profit on the transaction.

Actually, you might exercise the call if the stock were selling at only 42 when the option was due to expire, because you could at least save yourself from taking a complete loss on the $137.50 that you paid for the call. But obviously, you would have been better off if you hadn't bought it in the first place. Similarly, the buyer of a put would not stand to make any money on his transaction unless the stock dropped below 37⅛ (38½ less 1⅜).

The longer-term contracts are written on an entirely different basis. The put-and-call dealer doesn't ask for so many points above or below the market in these contracts; instead he guarantees to give you the stock (on a call) or take it from you (on a put) at the present market price. But for this guarantee he asks a considerably higher price — $300, $400, maybe $700 or more. The amount of this premium depends on the price of the stock and the record of its stability. He will charge more on a high-priced stock than a low one, more on one that has been fluctuating a lot than on one that has been pretty stable.

Obviously, if you pay $400 for a 90-day call on 100 shares of a stock, you don't stand to make a profit unless the stock rises by more than four points sometime in the three-month period.

As a general rule, long-terms calls cost fractionally more than puts in the same stock because of the long-term upward trend of the market.

Occasionally, a speculator will buy both a put and a call on the same stock and thus put himself in a position to jump either way should the market take a decided turn either up or down at any time during the life of his contract. Here, he has his choice of two kinds of contracts. He can buy a *straddle* in which both the put and the call are written on the basis of the current market price, or at a lower cost he can buy a *spread* in which the call will be a point or two above the market and the put a point or two below.

Sometimes if a man has a long-term straddle or spread he can be lucky enough to make money on both sides of it. Perhaps the market rises sharply — in which case he can make a profit by exercising his call — and then drops sharply, enabling him to make money on his put.

While put-and-call contract terms are fairly standard, some dealers frequently advertise special contracts which combine features of both the short- and long-term contracts. Thus, a dealer might advertise a call on a specific stock good for 70 days at a specific price 5 points above the current market, and at a premium of $150. This would mean that the stock would have to go up more than 6½ points within the 70 days or it would not be profitable for the buyer to exercise his call.

Puts and calls are not traded on any exchange. If you want to buy one, you can arrange for its purchase through your regular broker. This costs you nothing, because he is compensated for the order by the put-and-call dealer. But in addition to the premium that you pay the dealer for your contract, you will, if you are buying a call, have to pay state and federal transfer taxes; no taxes are levied on a put. Furthermore if you decide to exercise an option — either to buy the stock outright or to sell it at the price fixed in the contract — the purchase or sale will be handled by your regular broker who will earn a standard commission on the transaction.

Although your contract for a put or a call will be negotiated with one of the regular dealers, he is not as a rule the one who really carries the risk. If he writes a short-term call for you on Rod & Reel at 21½, he finds somebody else who will guarantee to deliver the stock at that price within thirty days and sells them the $137.50 contract for $112.50.

Who is this "somebody else"? It might be a wealthy individual, but more times than not it's likely to be an insurance company, a large trust, or a foundation — some agency with lots of capital and a big inventory of securities. Since only about 70% of all puts and calls are ever exercised, such agencies find that they can earn a good short-term return on their money with negligible risk in the long run by taking over the put-and-call dealer's risk.

Of the $25 spread which the dealer would realize on your Rod & Reel call ($137.50 less $112.50), he keeps $12.50 and splits the other half with your broker and the broker representing whoever takes the contract off the dealer's hands.

The direct speculative uses of a put or a call are fairly obvious. Their uses for protective purposes are not always so clear, but if a man has a substantial profit in a stock he owns and wants to protect it for a specified period, he can buy a put. Or if he is a short seller, he can buy a call to protect himself against a rising market.

He could, of course, achieve the same objective without spending any money by placing a stop order to sell or a stop order to buy, but this device might not be elastic enough for him. For instance, if a man had bought a stock at 60 and it were now selling at 70, he might buy a 60-day put at that price for $200 or so. But if he were to place a stop order on the same stock, he would have to pick a precise price at which he wanted to sell.

If, for instance, he placed a stop order at 68, it might happen that a brisk sell-off would hit the market and the stock would drop to 68, at which point he would be sold out. Then after the market recovered, perhaps only a few days later, the stock might be selling above 70 again, but he would no longer own it.

Instead of buying a put, he might sell his stock at 70 and buy a six-month call at 70 for perhaps $250 or $300. If the stock were to drop, the most he could lose would be the cost of the call. But if it were to continue rising, he would be in exactly the same position as if he still owned the stock.

Options have another distinct advantage to the speculator. A man can buy a call on a stock without tying up his money as he would have to do if he bought the same stock on margin. The same thing is true with respect to short selling. His actual out-of-pocket costs may be higher, operating on a put-and-call rather than a margin basis, but if there is a significant price movement in the stock, his profit may make the cost look incidental.

The juggling of these various speculative devices, weighing the risks and costs of each against the other, makes the business of professional speculation a highly complicated one. This alone can explain why it is probably true that more people who speculate lose money than make money.

But an even more important reason lies in the unwillingness of many a speculator to study thoroughly all of the facts about a company before he buys or sells its stock. Bernard M. Baruch, probably America's most successful speculator, made it an inviolable rule never to become involved in a speculative venture until he had mastered all the facts about it. As he once explained, successful speculation demands not only courage, persistence, and a judgment unclouded by emotion, but above all things it requires an infinite capacity for taking pains — the pains to analyze all available facts.

Chapter 22

How to Tell What the Market Is Doing

WHEN most people buy securities for the first time, they are apt to do it for the wrong reasons. They will buy a stock because they've heard other people, their friends or business associates, talk about it.

It seems to be human nature to believe that the other fellow always knows a good thing, that he has reliable inside information on how a company is doing.

Is there such a thing as *inside information?*

Of course there is.

The officers of a company know more about that firm and its prospects than anybody else could possibly know. And they have friends with whom they discuss their company's situation. In effect, those friends do have what appears to be privileged information — the real "inside."

Nevertheless, anyone who invests his money on the basis of what he thinks is an inside *tip* is apt to be seriously misled. Why?

Because no discreet company official — and most officials are necessarily prudent men — will ever reveal confidential information about a company or discuss the full facts about its situation, both the pros and the cons, publicly. If he talks about company affairs at all, he will probably talk only about those things that show how well the company's doing or expects to do. And by the time even this kind of information gets passed along from friend to friend until it reaches you, it may bear only scant relation to the facts. At that point, it can probably be defined only as gossip.

How, then, should a man set about investing?

If he doesn't know anything at all about the market or the stocks of various companies, where can he turn for information?

Probably the first and most obvious answer to that is the newspaper — one of the big metropolitan daily newspapers that carries complete stock market quotations and has a well-rounded coverage of financial news, or one of the four regional editions of the *Wall Street Journal.*

If he is not already familiar with the *stock tables,* probably his first step should be to study them regularly for a period of time. If he reads a morning paper, he will find the stocks traded during the preceding day on the New York Stock Exchange, listed in alphabetical order; the late edition of the evening paper provides that information for the stocks traded that same day.

If our Rod & Reel Company were sold on the Exchange, a complete entry for one day, with the appropriate column heads, might look like this:

Year to Date High	Low	Stocks & Dividend	Sales in 100s	Open	High	Low	Close	Net Change
42½	38¾	Rod & Reel 2	17	39¾	40¼	39⅝	40¼	+¾

The column heads make much of the information self-explanatory. Obviously, the stock has been traded in a fairly narrow range, having fluctuated only between a low of 38¾ and a high of 42½ all year. A comparison of this price range with the range recorded by other stocks will give you some general idea of whether Rod & Reel might be classified as an investment-type stock or a speculation. As a very rough rule of thumb, the greater the price fluctuation, the lower the investment caliber of the stock.

The dividend gives you another clue to the quality of the stock. With an annual dividend rate of $2 and a current price of $40, Rod & Reel is yielding exactly 5%, which in the years since the war would be considered fairly conservative. Very often after the dividend figure there will appear a small letter which will refer to a footnote. These footnotes can be very important, because they may indicate that the dividend figure includes extra dividends, or that this was the dividend paid last year, or that it represents only the total paid so far this year for a stock not on a regular dividend basis.

The figure for the number of shares traded simply shows how Rod & Reel stacks up alongside others as far as market interest is concerned. Sales volume of a stock in which there is considerable speculative interest will very often exceed that of some of the better-grade market leaders.

The open, high, low, and close figures give you a complete picture of how Rod & Reel moved during the trading day. Obviously in this case, it sold off a little bit after the opening and then recovered to close at the day's high. On any given day, the pattern of price movement will not be the same for all stocks — but this profile on Rod & Reel will show you whether its market performance is generally in line with that for the market as a whole. If Rod & Reel had opened at its low for the day and marched steadily along to close at its high, while the market as a whole declined from the open to the close, you could conclude that Rod & Reel had demonstrated a good deal of strength, because it ran counter to the downward trend.

The *net change* figure shows the difference between the closing price for one day and the closing price of the *preceding* day — not the difference between the opening and closing prices for the day. Yesterday's close may have been either higher or lower than today's opening.

Occasionally, you may notice that the price of a stock is down from the preceding day, but the net-change figure doesn't show a corresponding drop. That's because the stock is being sold *ex dividend*. Suppose Rod & Reel pays its quarterly dividend of 50¢ to stockholders on its books as of the close of business on Friday, September 15. Beginning Tuesday, September 12, and running through Friday, the stock will be worth 50¢ less, because anyone who buys it during that period will not be eligible for the dividend. This is so because it takes four days to make delivery of stock and only those people who actually own the stock on Monday, September 11, will be on the company's records Friday, September 15. When a stock is sold ex dividend, its price is expected to decline by the amount of the dividend, and if that is exactly what happens the net-change figure will show no gain or loss.

This four-day delivery interval is also important when a stock goes *ex rights*. Thus, a company with a new issue of additional stock might announce that stockholders as of Friday, September 15, would have the right to buy new stock in proportion to their present holdings at a price somewhat below the market. But obviously only those people who bought the stock on or before Monday, September 11, would appear on the company's records four days later, and anybody who bought the stock after that date wouldn't get the rights. Whenever a stock goes ex rights, it usually sells at a price that is lower by an amount roughly equal to the value of the rights. During the time that the rights can be exercised, they are bought and sold separately.

Obviously it would be a mistake to draw any positive conclusions about a stock on the basis of one day's trading pattern. But if you watch a stock over a period of time and compare it closely with a dozen or so others, particularly those in the same or a related field, you will begin to get an idea of how that stock is regarded by all the thousands of people whose transactions from day to day make the market.

In addition to the tables of prices on stocks traded that day, a few big-city newspapers also publish the bid-and-asked quotations on those stocks which are inactive. Even on an active day there are likely to be no trades at all in as many as one third of the stocks of the 1100 companies listed on the Big Board. The bid-and-asked quotations enable an owner to keep an eye on the price movements of his stock even though it isn't traded.

Not all newspapers publish anything like this complete information on Big Board stocks. In the smaller cities, the daily newspapers may list only 100 or so stocks and give only opening and closing prices on these, plus maybe the net change from the preceding day.

The Curb stocks don't get nearly as much play as those of the Big Board, and stocks listed on the other exchanges get press notice only in the areas where there is some public interest in them. Much the same standard determines just how many unlisted stocks are published and which ones.

Prices reported in the newspapers for bonds are apt to seem a little confusing. Although bonds are usually sold in $1000 units, their prices are quoted as though they had a $100 denomination. Thus a quotation of 98 would indicate an actual price of $980, and one of 98⅜ would be $983.75.

Since government bonds sold on the open market are traded not in eighths or quarters but in thirty-seconds, a special price-reporting formula has been developed for them. Thus a printed quotation of 99.16 actually means a price of $995. Here's how you arrive at that: that point isn't a decimal point; it is only a device for separating the round figure from the fraction. Hence the quotation really stands for 99¹⁶⁄₃₂, or 99½ or $995. Sometimes Treasuries are sold on a price change of just ¹⁄₆₄ rather than ¹⁄₃₂. If a plus sign appears after the published quotation for a government bond, this means that ¹⁄₆₄ should be added to the published price.

In addition to prices on individual security issues, almost every daily paper does publish some report on the average movement of New York Stock Exchange prices.

There are a number of these *averages* which are supposed

to serve as barometers of the business. Probably the best known of them is the Dow-Jones Average.

Actually, the Dow-Jones Average isn't one average but four — one for utilities, one for rails, one for industrials, and a composite one which is supposed to reflect conditions in all divisions of the market. These averages are computed five different times a day — at the end of every hour of trading on the New York Stock Exchange — and the index figures are flashed direct to stockbrokers, where they are posted on the quotation board.

The utility index is an average of prices for 15 utilities; the rail index covers 20 railroads; the industrial average is based on the stocks of 30 leading manufacturers and distributors; and the general index includes all 65.

Over the years, these averages have come to be accepted as the bible of the business, partly because the Dow-Jones Company, which originated them, is the publisher of the country's leading financial newspaper, the *Wall Street Journal*.

But in recent years the suspicion has grown that this bible is not divinely inspired, that the Dow-Jones Averages are not an infallible measure of the market. This criticism has been aimed especially at the Dow-Jones Industrial Average, probably the most important of them all, and it is based on two counts.

In the first place, it is argued that the 30 stocks which make up the index are not truly representative of all the industrials listed on the Big Board. They are definitely in the "blue chip" classification — stocks such as General Motors, American Telephone, Standard Oil of New Jersey, Du Pont, Allied Chemical and Dye, F. W. Woolworth, Eastman Kodak, Sears Roebuck, American Tobacco, General Electric, and General Foods.

In the second place, over the years many of these stocks have been split several times, and with each split the price of the stock has dropped proportionately. Thus, if the split were two-for-one, the price of the stock could be expected to decline about 50%; on a four-for-one split it would decline about 75%.

Since the Dow-Jones Averages are arrived at by adding the prices of all the stock together and dividing by their number, it is obvious that the price reductions resulting from such splits could throw the average seriously out of kilter. Dow-Jones has sought to correct such distortions by various mathematical formulas, but they haven't worked out too well. Those companies that have never split their stock still exert a stronger influence in the average than they should. Thus Allied Chemical & Dye exerts more influence than General Motors, despite the fact that the total value of all its outstanding stock is only about one seventh of General Motors.

As a result of its mathematical imperfections, the Dow-Jones Industrial Average can go up while the aggregate value of all of the shares of the stocks that comprise it goes down. This actually happens on occasion. For instance, on one particular day the Dow-Jones Average showed an increase of about ½ of 1%, but on that same day the actual value of all of the shares of the 30 companies dropped from 26½ to 25½ million. The apparent gain was all accounted for by a rise in the price of a few stocks that didn't have nearly as many shares outstanding as those companies whose stocks declined.

Other well-known daily stock market indexes are those compiled by the *New York Times,* the *New York Herald*

Tribune, and Standard & Poor's, the largest securities research organization in the business. Since the *Times* and *Herald Tribune* indexes are computed in something of the same way as the Dow-Jones, they are sometimes criticized on much the same grounds.

The Standard & Poor's Daily Index, for 90 stocks, however, is computed by a different system, which takes into account the total number of shares outstanding, as well as the price. As a consequence, this index is coming to be accepted as a more reliable barometer of the business, but Dow-Jones defenders claim it isn't sensitive enough. They say the Standard & Poor Index includes too many stocks, while the Dow-Jones Index, built principally on just the market leaders, shows the trend better since these are the stocks that first reflect any change in the wind.

The difference in computation can make for startling differences in results, particularly over a long period of time. Thus in mid-1952, the Standard & Poor's Industrial Index showed that stocks had passed their 1929 peak, thanks in part to the boom in oil stocks, heavily represented in that index, while the Dow-Jones Index showed industrials still lagging almost 30% behind that old record.

For many years to come, however, the Dow-Jones Averages will continue to be the ones most closely watched, not because they are necessarily the best but simply because they are the only ones computed on an hourly basis, and every man who wants to know how the market is doing at any given time of the day can call his broker and get the answer — an answer that may often be the one which makes him finally decide to buy or sell.

Chapter 23
Financial News and What to Make of It

ONCE a man starts following stock prices and averages it isn't long until he is reading the rest of the *financial section* of his newspaper.

Here, obviously, he will find much important information both about business in general and about individual companies — their plans for expansion, their new products, their sales and earnings records. Some of these news stories dealing with individual companies may be a little on the optimistic side, since they are often based on publicity releases furnished by the companies themselves, but every responsible newspaper today makes an effort to be as objective as possible in the handling of such news.

A standard feature of the financial section in every big city newspaper is the daily column in which the action of the stock market is reported and often analyzed in terms of various technical factors — the primary trend, the secondary movement, the resistance levels, and so on.

While it is unquestionably true that there are technical factors in the market that do affect its direction over short periods of time, these are conditions which are apt to be of far greater importance to the professional trader or speculator than to the average investor, especially the newcomer who may be understandably confused by some reference to a "double top" or "dormant bottom."

Again, technical market factors are not apt to be as significant even to the daily trader as they were in the days when margin buying and short selling were more important and before the Securities & Exchange Commission put a stop to all efforts at manipulating the market.

Nevertheless, the market columns can make interesting reading after one gets used to the jargon, and soon even the neophyte finds himself acquiring some familiarity with such phrases as "technically strong" or "technically weak," the "short interest" and "the Dow theory."

The phrases *technically strong* or *technically weak* do have fairly precise meanings. Suppose stock prices have been moving more or less steadily upward over a long period of time. Inevitably in such a bull market movement, there are price advances and price reactions, ups and downs in the market. If the volume of sales is heavy when stocks go up and light when they go down during a bull movement, the market can be described as technically strong. Conversely, in a long downward trend, if volume is heavy on the down side and light on the rallies, the market is technically weak. This interpretation is based on the theory that sales volume always shows the dominant trend.

The term *short interest,* as applied most usually to the New York Stock Exchange, refers to the total number of shares of Big Board stocks that all the sellers are short; they have sold the stock but must still buy it back to cover their positions. No short sale, of course, can be made without a broker's knowledge, and hence a broker always knows the total number of shares that his customers are short in every stock. Once a month, member firms report these figures to the Exchange, and the Exchange makes a public report on the short interest in every stock where it is an item of consequence. Not once since the depression has the total short interest exceeded $\frac{1}{10}$ of 1% of all shares outstanding.

Nevertheless, when there is a sizable short interest, the market is generally considered to be in a strong position. This may seem strange, but the fact of the matter is that that short interest does represent a cushion of buy orders. Those men who are short stock are ultimately going to have to buy, and their buying will help stabilize the market, force it up.

The *Dow theory* is at once the most celebrated, complicated, and least understood interpretation of market action, probably because neither Charles Dow, who founded the Dow-Jones Company, nor any of his various disciples have ever defined the theory precisely.

In essence, the Dow theorists hold that there is a primary movement in the market at all times — a kind of basic tidal action. Then there's a secondary movement which might be likened to waves. And finally there are the ripples on the surface that represent the daily movement of prices. They contend that it is possible to tell when either the primary or secondary directions change by comparing the actions of the industrial and rail averages — Dow-Jones Averages, of course. When both of them move in the same direction for a given period of time, either notably up or down, they are supposed to indicate a significant change in the direction of the market which will hold good until the two averages "confirm" each other again in an opposite direction.

This is what the learned market experts are talking about when they say "the rails confirmed the industrials" — or didn't.

Dow theorists contend that by their somewhat nebulous formula they have been able to forecast almost every significant movement in the market for many years. Other analysts, looking at the same set of facts, dispute the Dow theory's record. They say it can only be made to look good when the forecasting has become history. Nevertheless, many financial editors continue to expound the Dow theory, and at least one company, Rhea, Greiner & Company of Colorado Springs, has a regular letter service (price $40 a year) analyzing the market about every ten days in Dow theory terms.

Very often in the reading of his newspaper, the new investor will encounter what appears to be a striking contradiction between the news and the market reaction to that news.

A company declares a special dividend — and its stock drops in price.

Sales of automobiles show surprising strength for some months — but motor stocks remain sluggish all through this period.

Congress enacts a new tax bill which lightens the tax burden on business — and the day it is passed, stocks sell off.

There is one simple explanation for these paradoxes: The stock market has "*discounted*" *the news*. The big traders, the people supposedly in the know, were sure that special dividend was coming, because the company's profits had been increasing spectacularly. The strong demand for new automobiles didn't surprise them; they had been expecting it. And as for the tax legislation favorable to business, they would have been surprised if Congress hadn't enacted it.

So frequently does this kind of thing happen that some people consider the market an infallible barometer of general business. They say that you can tell what's going to happen to business by the way the stock market acts.

Actually, this theory doesn't stand the light of investigation, and those who hold to it have a tall job of explaining to do if they try to account for even a few of the most glaring exceptions.

For instance, business conditions began to look a little less than rosy in the late spring and summer of 1929, but it was not until October 23 of that year that the market hit the big slide, with typical stocks slumping 100 points or more in four successive trading sessions as more than forty million shares of stock changed hands.

More recently the stock market has performed no better as a guide to our economic health; since the end of World War II, it has missed the boat on every important turn in business.

Thus, in 1945, business was retarded by the necessity of reconverting from war to peace, but the stock market kept boiling happily along until September 1946, then slumped when business had already begun to improve. Business continued steadily on the upgrade for several years, but the market didn't catch up with this change of direction until early 1949.

One economist who made a study of the correlation between business and the stock market concluded that, as a forecaster of business, the stock market was right just about 50% of the time. In other words, you'd be just as well off if you flipped a coin as you would if you studied the market averages in trying to decide whether business would improve or decline.

But if the stock market doesn't anticipate business, it must sooner or later fall into step with the basic business trends, because in the end stock values are determined by our economic health. That's why the investor is well advised to keep his eye on some of the more basic *indexes* of business such as the Federal Reserve Board index of production and various indexes on steel output, carloadings, department store sales, and unfilled orders and prices, both for farm goods and industrial raw materials. These will tell him how much America is producing, how rapidly this output is moving into the channels of distribution, and what kind of consumer demand there is for it. In the long run, these are the vital factors that will determine the real value of the stock that you own in any company — how much the company is likely to earn and what kind of dividend it can pay.

Obviously, if he reads the financial pages of his newspaper, the investor will gain something of an insight into what's happening to business. But the daily reports often lack continuity. The reader is unable to see the forest for the trees.

To provide the reader with a long-range perspective, many newspapers now publish a business column as well as a financial column. One of the best of these is "The Business Outlook," published in the *Philadelphia Bulletin* and syndicated in a number of other newspapers.

However, many an investor who wants to be sure that he has a solid and well-balanced view of the business scene finds it desirable to subscribe to some specialized publication, such as the daily *Wall Street Journal* ($20 a year), or *Business Week* ($6). And because political developments are increasingly important in the conduct of business affairs, the *Kiplinger Washington Letter* ($18) and the *Whaley-Eaton American Letter* ($25) are also widely read by investors.

Still others look to Washington for another reason: because various government publications provide the most authoritative data about business conditions, however dully, at the lowest cost. Most noteworthy of these are two publications of the Department of Commerce — the *Survey of Current Business* ($3.25 a year) and *Economic Indicators* ($1.75), a monthly collection of the most basic statistics about business in chart form. The Federal Reserve Board's monthly *Bulletin* ($2) is another important and reliable source of information about our economic health.

In addition to general business publications there are, of course, the financial magazines — *Barron's* ($12), *Financial World* ($20), *Forbes* ($5) and the *Magazine of Wall Street* ($15) — that undertake to appraise the business situation primarily in terms of stock market values.

Perhaps as helpful a publication as any in this business and financial field is *The Exchange,* which is published monthly by the New York Stock Exchange and costs the subscriber only $1 a year.

Another very useful publication of the Stock Exchange is a quarterly pamphlet entitled *Investment Facts About Common Stocks* which lists the hundreds of stocks that have paid dividends without ever missing a one for at least 20 years — some for 50 years, a few even for 100 years. These are the "blue chip" stocks, and the booklet gives not only their dividend history but their current prices and dividend rates. There is no charge for this booklet. You can probably get a copy from your broker, but if he doesn't have one, just write to the Exchange and ask for it.

But all of these publications and services leave the investor, in the final analysis, to work out his own destiny. They give him basic information, but they don't tell him what to do about it.

Chapter 24
Financial Advice — At a Price

DO you want help with your investment problem — information, advice, recommendations?

You can get it — at a price. Whether it's worth the price you pay is something else again.

Maybe you want something more than advice. Maybe you don't want to worry about your investment problem at all. If that's the case — and if you have about $100,000 to invest, preferably a good deal more — you can turn the whole matter over to some top-flight *investment counselor* whose sole business is that of guiding the investment destiny of his clients — making all the buying and selling decisions for them and seeing that they are properly executed by a brokerage firm. There are more than one hundred of these counseling firms that spend their full time investing other people's money — for a fee, of course — in New York City alone, and there are many others in all the major cities from Coast to Coast.

In the main, these investment counselors do a sound job for their clients, mostly big institutions, but their services are obviously beyond the reach of the average investor. So what can he do? Isn't there somebody willing to help him?

Indeed yes. There are dozens of *investment advisory services,* all only too willing to help him, and they offer him a bewildering array of publications and services. Some are simply compilations of statistical information. Some undertake to review business conditions as they affect the investment outlook. Some provide recommendations about hundreds of different securities — what to buy, what to sell, what to hold. Some, believing that good investment advice can't be turned out on a mass-production basis, undertake to provide a kind of tailor-made service; they offer to answer inquiries and to permit occasional consultation with their experts. And some even offer a reasonably well-rounded counseling service available at a negotiated fee to the smaller investor, perhaps the man with only $25,000 to invest in securities.

Some of the financial advisory organizations have for sale all of these different kinds of services, while others offer only one kind or another.

Most controversial of all the services are those that undertake to give advice about the market, usually in a weekly letter, sold on a subscription basis. Many of these publications have their own rating service covering hundreds of different stocks that tell the subscriber whether to buy or sell, and most of them maintain *supervised lists* of those investments that they consider particularly attractive. In effect, these supervised lists are supposed to represent model investment programs.

Most of these services are more concerned about the short-term outlook — what the market is likely to do in the next couple of months — than they are with the problem of long-term investment. A few of them even limit themselves almost exclusively to a discussion of technical factors in the market.

There is one other common characteristic which these serv-

HOW TO BUY STOCKS

ices share: They will all tell you how successful they've been in calling the turns in the market and in recommending good buys and good sells at just the strategic moment.

Actually, how good are they?

There's no easy answer to that, because there is no way to compute and compare their batting averages. Some make flat-footed recommendations and some hedge their suggestions with all kinds of qualifications. However, one stock market analyst who did keep check on 16 services for a period of years found that if an investor had followed all their 7500 different recommendations, he would have ended up just 1.43% worse than the market averages.

Here are some of the best-known services of all kinds.

Companies rendering a comprehensive research and advisory service:

The Big Three of the financial research business are:

STANDARD & POOR'S CORPORATION, 345 HUDSON STREET, NEW YORK 14

MOODY'S INVESTORS SERVICE, 65 BROADWAY, NEW YORK 6

FITCH INVESTORS SERVICE, 120 WALL STREET, NEW YORK 5

Known primarily as publishers of financial data, these three firms supply the entire investment business, including all the other advisory services, with the basic facts and figures on all securities sold in the public market and on the companies that issue them. Many of their publications, such as those dealing exclusively with bonds, are too specialized to be of significance to the average investor, but both he and his broker would be utterly lost if it were not for the complete and detailed information which these organizations supply on stocks, both listed and unlisted.

Much of the research material supplied by one firm is also supplied by both or either of its competitors, but they use different methods of organizing and publishing the material.

Most fundamental of all the reference books are Standard & Poor's *Corporation Records* and Moody's *Manuals*. In these massive volumes, running into tens of thousands of pages, you'll find a brief history of every publicly owned company in the United States and full financial data running back over a period of years — figures on assets, income, earnings, dividends, and stock prices.

Standard & Poor's keeps its six-volume *Corporation Records* up to date with daily supplements that summarize important developments affecting various companies, while Moody's uses a twice-a-week report for its *Manuals* on industrials, railroads, and utilities. Standard & Poor's also has a special service reviewing conditions industry by industry. These industry surveys cover developments in 1000 different companies.

These services, the backbone of the securities research business, are far too costly for most individuals. Nor is it necessary for a man to spend a couple of hundred dollars a year on them, since he can usually refer to them in his broker's office, or his registered representative can get for him the information he wants on any company.

All three of the agencies, for instance, have a bulletin service on all the leading companies. In these bulletins, all the essential facts about a company are condensed onto a single sheet of paper about the size of this page, and all of them give some sort of opinion or evaluation of the company's stock. Most brokers subscribe to one or all of these services and make the data freely available to their customers or prospective customers.

Even more condensed information is provided in the pocket-size manuals prepared by Fitch and Standard & Poor. Here the investor can find the monthly high-and-low prices over the past year or so, the high and low for the past dozen years, and current data on assets, earnings, and dividends for all stocks listed on the New York Stock and Curb Exchanges, plus about 1200 unlisted securities. New editions both of Fitch's *Stock Record* and Standard & Poor's *Stock Guide* are issued monthly, and both services are priced at $24 a year. Many brokers give occasional free copies of these manuals to their customers and prospects.

For the individual investor, both Standard & Poor's and Moody's have special services and letters that comment on business developments as they affect the outlook for individual stocks and industries. Standard & Poor's has its weekly *Outlook,* a 10-page magazine ($65 a year), a daily *Facts and Forecast Service* ($150), and an *Investment Advisory Survey* ($65), which consists of an 8-page confidential bulletin featuring a supervised list of recommended investments; subscribers are offered an inquiry and consultation service.

Moody's *Stock Survey,* a 12-page weekly letter, reviews market conditions and analyzes various investment opportunities ($120 a year). Around this survey and its bulletins on individual companies, Moody's has built an Investors Advisory

Service, offering subscribers a review of their present holdings plus recommendations about what to buy or sell. (Price: $160 for a portfolio of 15 stocks or less, $2 for each additional stock.)

Finally, all three of the services — Standard & Poors, Moody's, and Fitch's — offer an individual investment counseling service at an annual retainer fee.

Chart services:

M. C. HORSEY & CO., 37 WALL STREET, NEW YORK 5

F. W. STEPHENS, 15 WILLIAM STREET, NEW YORK 5

Both of these companies publish chart books which graphically portray the monthly movement of prices and sales volume over a period of years for individual stocks, a separate chart for each stock. Stephens's *Graphic Stocks* covers 1001 stocks and usually shows a 10-year movement. Price: $50 a year for six isues or $10 a copy. Horsey's *Stock Picture,* also issued bimonthly, covers 1200 stocks and a 15-year period. Price: $60 a year or $12 a copy.

Companies offering business and investment advisory services:

ALEXANDER HAMILTON INSTITUTE, 71 WEST 23D STREET,
NEW YORK 10

The Business Conditions Service offered by this well-known organization is built primarily around its *Weekly Bulletin,* a report on key economic factors, plus news notes on individual industries and significant political developments. Additionally, subscribers also receive a *Weekly Investment Bulletin,* which, in addition to the usual market comment, rates 500 stocks, and gives specific recommendations to buy, hold, or sell. Three or four noteworthy stocks are discussed in greater detail. The service includes other *Bulletins* on commodities, on credit and sales, and on new products or business developments. Subscribers are entitled to ask advice about their own situation. Price: $48 a year to new subscribers, $35 to former subscribers.

AMERICAN INSTITUTE FOR ECONOMIC RESEARCH, GREAT BARRINGTON, MASSACHUSETTS

This nonprofit, noncommercial foundation undertakes to make the results of its fundamental research in economics available to the average man at cost. Its weekly *Research Report* reviews in chart and text the most basic factors affecting supply, demand, and prices. Its semi-monthly *Investment Bulletin* covers three typical investment plans, designed for different objectives, and recommends specific securities for each plan, with reasons why. These plans are designed for long-term investment, and the Foundation does not attempt to forecast short swings or technical movements. Additionally, the Institute publishes basic studies on inflation, life insurance, investment trusts, social security, and the like, usually available at $1 each. Prices: Sustaining membership, including all publications, $35 a year. *Investment Bulletin* alone, $10 a year.

AMERICAN INVESTORS SERVICE, LARCHMONT, NEW YORK

On the assumption that most market moves are generated by conditions within the market itself rather than by economic factors, the weekly *Market Trend Analysis* and *Stock Selection Reports* of this service focus primarily on matters of timing and selection as influenced by technical conditions. However involved these considerations may be, the service reduces them all to a series of specific recommendations about what stocks to buy; thereafter these are marked hold, until a specific sell recommendation is made. Price $100 a year, $5 for a five-week trial. American Investors also renders an Account Management Service under which it assumes complete responsibility for a client's portfolio. Costs begin at ½ of 1% a year on holdings worth only $20,000 and are graduated down to ¼ of 1% on holdings in excess of $200,000.

MAJOR L. L. B. ANGAS, INC., 480 LEXINGTON AVE., NEW YORK 17

Probably the most colorful and controversial figure in the forecasting business, Major Angas places primary reliance on a psychological evaluation of the public temper toward the market, as he appraises it. His *Digests* deal with timing and strategy as they relate both to long-term and intermediate trends in the general market. Ten or more of them are issued every year, not on any regular schedule but as market conditions warrant. Additionally, he has a wire service, offering subscribers a 30-word night letter, giving an advance summary of any new buy or sell recommendations in his *Digests;*

these are sent collect. The subscribers may also send him six prepaid wire inquiries a year. The *Digests* and the wires are both confined to general market action, and no advice is given on individual stocks. Price: *Digests,* $25 a year; Wire Service, $25 a year; combination rate, $30.

BABSON'S REPORTS, WELLESLEY HILLS 82, MASSACHUSETTS

One of the best publicized of all financial services, the weekly *Babson Report,* which comments on business and political news as well as on the outlook for individual companies, is really only a part of the service which the subscriber buys. His investment situation is analyzed, purchases or sales are suggested, and the subscriber gets a one-page report on each company whose stock he owns — a red-bordered report if Babson's thinks it bears close watching, a green border if all is clear. As long as he subscribes, he gets all new reports on these companies (with appropriate borders) as they are issued — at least once a year, more often if conditions warrant. Babson's service is designed for the investor who has at least $10,000, half of which he can put into stocks. Price $138 a year.

BONDEX, 25 BROAD STREET, NEW YORK 4

The *Stock Market Bulletin* and the *Market Coordinator,* now available to individuals, were formerly sold by Bondex only as part of its Bankers' Investment Service which covers government, municipal, and corporate bonds as well. The *Co-*

ordinator provides a brief weekly comment on all these securities, but the investor is apt to be much more interested in the more exhaustive *Stock Market Bulletin,* also published weekly. A technical service, the Bulletin interprets virtually all business and economic news in terms of its market impact. Bondex has its own index of market health, which it relies on for buy and sell signals. It also recommends stocks for investment and for growth and comments on situations for short-term trading profits. Price: $50 a year.

BROOKMIRE INVESTORS SERVICE, 52 WALL STREET, NEW YORK 5

A weekly bulletin or letter analyzes and forecasts the market, comments on individual companies, and reports on the status of the 42 stocks included in its managed list for different investment objectives. Subscription includes special reports on individual industries and market situations. Price: $36 a year, $10 a quarter.

INTERNATIONAL SECURITIES BUREAU, 350 FIFTH AVENUE, NEW YORK 1

In the publication of its weekly *Selected Securities Guide,* the Bureau draws on the business information which it gathers for its other specialized services covering such fields as textiles, housing, distribution. In addition to news reports on individual securities, the *Guide* makes specific recommendations on what to buy or sell and when to do it. Ratings on individual stocks indicate prices at which they may be considered cheap or overvalued for either long-term or short-term holdings. The subscriber also receives quarterly a supervised list of securities (Price: $72 a year). The Bureau also publishes a *Business and Investment Service* which provides more basic information on business and market trends, and the subscriber to this service gets the Bureau's other services — the *Guide,* the supervised list, and a weekly report on foreign affairs — at a price of $100 a year.

INVESTOGRAPHS, 31 GIBBS STREET, ROCHESTER 4, NEW YORK

In addition to a fundamental analysis of business trends affecting sales, profit margins, and earnings, the Investograph *Weekly Letter* comments on technical conditions in the market with special reference to volume as the key indicator of public confidence in the market. Price: $60 a year, $36 for six months, $18 for three. Since 1930, the company has also supplied an Investograph Service which undertakes to present in easily read charts the key fundamentals from income statements and balance sheets that affect the value of a given stock. Price for 300 corporations, $130 or $157 in combination with the *Letter,* for 140 corporations, $95 or $119 in combination. A still more technical service, *Action-Reaction Signals,* is offered at $335 a year.

STUDLEY, SHUPERT & CO., 24 FEDERAL STREET, BOSTON 10, MASSACHUSETTS

The *Common Stock Summary,* published six times a year at an annual subscription price of $150, provides detailed statistical data in a form that can be easily assimilated on more than 400 leading companies, divided into two dozen industrial groups. For each company, the *Summary* traces the pattern of earnings, dividends, and prices over various intervals of time, showing the worst years and the best years in the several periods. Data are also supplied on working capital and book value. The firm also has an Industrial Service providing more detailed information on each company at an annual cost of $500 and a comparable service on 175 public utilities at $400.

UNITED BUSINESS AND INVESTMENT SERVICE, 210 NEWBURY ST., BOSTON 16, MASSACHUSETTS

Each issue of its comprehensive *Weekly Report* contains a review of the business outlook, a report on Washington developments, a forecast of commodity prices, an appraisal of the stock market, and specific recommendations for buying or selling different stocks. Regular reports are made on all stocks that are kept on its supervised lists. Periodic features include analyses of individual stocks and groups of stocks, a report on bonds, various statistical indexes of business, and a summary of the opinion of eight other advisory services. Subscribers are offered an inquiry and advisory service. Price: $60 a year, $32 for six months.

THE VALUE LINE, 350 MADISON AVENUE, NEW YORK 17

Value Line takes the standard chart on what has happened to each of 320 leading stocks and then adds a line which shows the subscriber exactly where this service thinks that stock is likely to go in the next year on the basis of what it considers to be the fundamental values involved. There's a chart on each stock once a quarter. Additionally, the subscriber gets a report on 60 stocks — "special situations" — not included in the 320. Other bonuses: a fortnightly letter of comment on the market and business, a report on Value Line's model fund, and lists of stocks that look like good buys. Price: $120 a year.

Chapter 25
How Your Broker Can Help You

IN the last analysis, the best answer that any investor can find to the problem of what stocks to buy is likely to be the answer that he works out for himself through study and investigation.

But where, you ask, can the average man who is willing to do his own investigating turn for the facts and the information he needs? The answer to that is — his broker.

Perhaps you think this is dubious advice. After all, isn't a broker interested in selling securities? Yes, a broker is a salesman. But that doesn't mean that your interests and his are completely opposed. Quite the contrary. Any salesman of any product wants his customer to be satisfied, because that's the best way of building his own business. That's especially true of the broker.

Then, too, there's an important difference between him and other salesmen. The automobile salesman wants to sell you a particular car. The insurance salesman wants to sell you a policy in his company. The salesman for a financial advisory service wants to sell you that service and nothing else.

As far as his own commission is concerned, the broker doesn't care which Big Board stocks you buy. He has essentially no ax to grind, at least as far as listed securities are concerned, because he stands to make about the same commission on the same total investment. When it comes to over-the-counter stocks, admittedly he could have, even though he knows better than anyone else that such a self-seeking policy would be bad business in the long run.

But how competent is the broker or his registered representative to give advice about your money and how to invest it?

Obviously that's a question to which there is no absolute answer. Nobody could possibly contend that all the tens of thousands of men in the business are pre-eminently well qualified to give investment help. Some are and some aren't.

But this much can be said: As a general rule, there isn't anybody to whom you can go who is apt to be nearly as well qualified — not your banker, not your lawyer, and certainly not just a business associate or the fellow in the club car.

After all, the registered representative works at the job of investing at least seven hours a day, five days a week, and he has been doing it for years. He has facts, figures, and information at his finger tips that nobody else can lay hold of easily. He has easy access to the basic reference works — Standard *Corporation Records* or Moody's *Manuals* — and he can make available to you detailed data about any publicly owned company in the United States. And in many brokerage firms he has behind him a well-qualified *research department*.

These research departments keep a close watch on news developments that affect securities, particularly those securities in which there is the greatest public interest. They subscribe to dozens of business and industrial publications as well as some of the more reliable financial advisory services. They conduct on-the-spot investigations of company operations, and they check frequently with the officials of those companies. They prepare analyses of important developments affecting various industries and companies, some for public distribution and some simply to keep their own registered representatives posted. These research reports are a far cry from the old *"broker's letter,"* a catch-as-catch-can commentary on business and the market, liberally interspersed with tips about what to buy or what to sell.

In their public advertisements some brokerage firms offer the services of their research department to present customers or prospective investors who may want to submit their whole investment situation for review. They offer to analyze present security holdings and make recommendations for purchases or sales without charge. Others ask a fee for such service that varies with the complexity of the individual problem.

How much you lean on your broker for help is up to you. You can in special circumstances give him a power of attorney to make all buying and selling decisions for you, but most brokers are loath to accept such complete *discretionary* authority. They prefer to act on your specific instructions. One thing you can be sure of: Lacking such instructions, no reputable broker, no member firm of the New York Stock Exchange, is going to "put you into" some stock or "sell you out" of it.

As a general rule, the registered representative today doesn't want to manage your investment affairs, and to be quite honest about it, he doesn't even want to tell you how to manage them.

He'll be glad to get you the facts and figures you need and to help you interpret them, but he prefers that the decisions about what to buy and what to sell be wholly your own. For one thing, you'll be less inclined to blame him for whatever might go wrong if you do determine your own investment course. More importantly, he knows that in the long run you are going to be a better and more successful investor. You'll have a greater interest in the problem and you'll be more willing to work at the job of investing.

Remember, every time somebody buys a stock, somebody else sells it. It's a difference of opinion that makes the market. If your opinions are better grounded in fact than the other fellow's, you are going to be right more often than he is. It's just that simple — and that complex.

Chapter 26
Can You "Beat the Market"?

ISN'T there any system to "beat the market," any system that will protect you against price fluctuations and virtually guarantee you a profit over the long pull?

Yes, there are such systems, and they work pretty well. However, they are far from foolproof, and they are not especially well adapted to the little investor. But at least they do point some important lessons about successful investing. They are called dollar averaging and formula investing.

Dollar averaging simply involves putting the same fixed amount of money — $200, $500, $1000 — into the same stock, regardless of its price movement, at regular intervals — say every six months — over a long period of time.

Following this system, you could have made a profit on probably 90% of the stocks listed on the New York Stock Exchange over almost any fifteen-year period you might want to pick.

Dollar averaging works simply because you buy more shares of a stock with your fixed amount of money when the stock is low in price than you do when it is comparatively high, and when the stock rises again you make a profit on the greater number of shares you got at low cost.

Suppose you bought $500 worth of a given stock when it

was selling at $10 a share, another $500 worth six months later when it was $9, another $500 worth at $8, and so on while the stock fell to $5, then rose to $15, and settled back to $10. If you then sold out, you would be able to show a profit of about 10%, despite the fact that you paid an average price of $10 and sold out at exactly that same price. You don't believe it?

Don't bother to figure it out, because here's the proof. Since you can't buy fractional shares of stock, it is assumed that at every different price level the buyer would purchase whatever number of shares would yield a total cost nearest $500.

Price per Share	Number of Shares Purchased	Cost of Shares	Number of Shares Owned	Cumulative Cost of Shares	Total Value of Shares
$10	50	$500	50	$ 500	$ 500
9	55	495	105	995	945
8	63	504	168	1499	1344
7	71	497	239	1996	1673
6	84	504	323	2500	1938
5	100	500	423	3000	2115
6	84	504	507	3504	3042
7	71	497	578	4001	4046
8	63	504	641	4505	5128
9	55	495	696	5000	6264
10	50	500	746	5500	7460
11	45	495	791	5995	8701
12	42	504	833	6499	9996
13	38	494	871	6993	11323
14	36	504	907	7497	12698
15	33	495	940	7992	14100
14	36	504	976	8496	13664
13	38	494	1014	8990	13182
12	42	504	1056	9494	12672
11	45	495	1101	9989	12111
10	50	500	1151	10489	11510

All told, you paid $10,489, and your holdings are worth $11,510.

And exactly the same results — exclusive of all dividends and purchase costs — would be achieved if the stock first rose from $10 to $15, then dropped to $5, then came back to $10. Here are the figures on that:

Price per Share	Number of Shares Purchased	Cost of Shares	Number of Shares Owned	Cumulative Cost of Shares	Total Value of Shares
$10	50	$500	50	$ 500	$ 500
11	45	495	95	995	1045
12	42	504	137	1499	1644
13	38	494	175	1993	2275
14	36	504	211	2497	2954
15	33	495	244	2992	3660
14	36	504	280	3496	3920
13	38	494	318	3990	4134
12	42	504	360	4494	4320
11	45	495	405	4989	4455
10	50	500	455	5489	4550
9	55	495	510	5984	4590
8	63	504	573	6488	4584
7	71	497	644	6985	4508
6	84	504	728	7489	4368
5	100	500	828	7989	4140
6	84	504	912	8493	5472
7	71	497	983	8990	6881
8	63	504	1046	9494	8368
9	55	495	1101	9989	9909
10	50	500	1151	10489	11510

There's only one significant difference between the two tables. Note that you are considerably better off all the way along the line if your stock drops first and then comes back.

Thus, in the first table, after the stock had fallen to $5 and recovered to $10, you could have sold out and made a profit of $1960 or almost 35% on your money.

So if the stock you buy drops in price and you have the confidence to believe that it will come back, as stocks in general always have, you would do well to continue buying it as it slides on down. This is called *"averaging down,"* and it's a concept which the investor who thinks the market is "too high to buy right now" might well keep in mind.

While no stock could ever follow the precise pattern set in the tables, the examples do serve to demonstrate the validity of the dollar averaging principle.

There's only one big catch to this system of beating the market. You've got to have the cash — yes, and the courage, too — to buy the same dollar amount of the stock at whatever interval of time you've fixed on, be it every six months, three months, or year.

And if it drops, you've got to keep right on buying in order to pick up the low-cost shares on which you can later make your profit. Unfortunately, when the stock market is down, the average man's bank account is likely to be down too, and so he often can't afford to buy at just the time he should.

That's why dollar averaging is a better system for the rich man to use than it is for the modest investor.

If this system had been applied to the 50 stocks in Standard & Poor's daily industrial average, the investor, starting in 1929 — about as bad a time as possible — would have seen the value of his investment double by 1952. Furthermore, he would have received dividends almost equal to his total investment. Only in the first years of the plan's operation would he have sustained an actual out-of-pocket loss.

Formula investing is not so much a system for beating the market as it is a mechanical means for enforcing prudence and caution. There are many different formula plans — almost every expert has his own — but stripped of their technicalities all of them can be reduced to the basic premise that an investment fund should be balanced between stocks and bonds, and that the ratio of the one kind of security to the other should be changed as the market rises and falls. You buy bonds and sell stocks when the market gets high, and you reverse the procedure when the market is low.

The premise is basically sound, but again, it's one that the average investor can't apply very effectively, since his investment fund is rarely large enough to make the purchase of any bonds feasible, except E bonds, on which little interest is paid in the first few years. However, savings bank deposits can be substituted for bond purchases whenever they are in order without serious loss of effectiveness.

To illustrate how a formula plan works, the investor starts out with 50% of his money in stocks and 50% in bonds. Whenever stock prices decline 20%, he sells bonds and uses the proceeds to buy stocks until he has restored the exact 50–50 balance, half of his money in each. If stock prices rise 25%, he sells stocks and buys bonds until he has again struck the 50–50 balance. He makes no change in his portfolio except at those two points — when stocks drop 20% or when they advance 25%.

This is the most elementary kind of formula plan, and an

investment counselor responsible for the conservative management of a large fund might insist on further refinements that would make it even less speculative. For instance, he might insist that no more than 5% of the total value of the fund be switched at any time from bonds to stocks, no matter how much stocks declined, without a waiting period of some months to see if the level of stock prices still indicated a greater switch from bonds into stocks. Again, he might decide that no money should ever be shifted from bonds into stocks at a time when the Federal Reserve Board's index of production showed a drop in manufacturing activity.

Formula investing can show amazing results. Thus a well-operated plan constructed along just these lines actually showed a profit over a tough 12-year period in which the Dow-Jones Averages declined 52%.

The formula idea got a terrific boost in 1938 when Vassar College announced that it would apply such a plan to the management of a big slice of its endowment fund. The *Vassar Plan* was pegged to the Dow-Jones Average. Starting with a 50–50 ratio, half the money in stocks and half in bonds, the plan provided for shifting by degrees into stocks when the Dow-Jones Averages declined until the fund would be 100% in stocks if there was as much as a 20-point drop in the Averages. Conversely the fund would be transferred into all bonds and no stocks if the Averages rose 60 points above the starting point.

A year after the Vassar plan, Yale came along with another one — a more conservative, less elastic plan — and formula investing had definitely made a niche for itself in the investment world, even though neither plan was sufficiently flexible to permit its sponsors to cash in as heavily as they might have on the postwar boom in common stocks, and some modification of the original formulas became necessary.

While the average investor might not be able to apply any neatly devised mathematical formula to his own situation, he can profit by paying heed to the one basic precept of all these formulas: Keep an eye on those market averages, and as they rise, let them act as a brake on your buying enthusiasm. Remember, no bull market movement lasts forever.

Chapter 27
Should You Buy a Mutual Fund?

THINKING is always hard work. Thinking about an investment problem is doubly hard because it frequently involves dealing with words and ideas that are somewhat strange.

In a situation like that it's a real temptation to let somebody else do your thinking for you.

And that's just what thousands of new investors have done in the last ten years. They have turned to the *investment trust* — especially the mutual fund — as the answer to all their investment problems. But many of them have found it to be not quite the perfect panacea that they thought it was.

There's no special magic about an investment trust — nor anything mysterious about its operation. Suppose you and some of your friends — twenty of you, all told — each have $1000 to spare. Instead of each of you investing your own money, you might decide to pool it and turn the whole sum over to one individual or manager to invest for you.

In that situation, the twenty of you would constitute an investment trust in miniature.

Now let's assume you're lucky and that at the end of the first year the manager of your little trust is able to report that he has made money for you. The value of the stocks which the trust owns has risen from $20,000 to $22,000. Each of your shares in that trust is now worth $1100 ($22,000 divided by 20).

You've been so successful, as a matter of fact, that some of your other friends would like to join your little trust. The twenty of you must now make one of two decisions.

You can decide that you're going to restrict the trust just to the original members and their original capital. If that's what you decide, you will have become a *closed-end trust.* There will be no new members or shareholders in your trust, unless, of course, one of the original twenty wants to sell his share to somebody else for whatever he can get for it. That's a right all of you always have.

Or you can decide to expand your trust and take in new members. Since your own shares are now worth $1100 apiece, you decide to allow them to buy in on that basis — $1100. When they put their new capital in, it will be invested as your original capital was, and all of you, the new and the old owners, will participate, share-and-share alike, in whatever profits the fund may make from now on.

And if still other people decide they'd like to buy a share in your trust at any future time, you decide to admit them at a price representing the trust's *net asset value per share.* This is determined by dividing the total value of the trust's holdings by the number of shares already outstanding.

If you decide to operate on this pattern, you will have become an *open-end trust,* or what is known more popularly today as a *mutual fund*.

This, in theory, is the essential difference between the closed-end and open-end trusts. In actuality, there are other differences.

Closed-end trusts are stock companies whose shares are bought and sold just like other stocks. The business of these trusts is investing, instead of manufacturing or merchandising, but they are operated just like any other company by officers and directors responsible to the shareholders.

Some of these companies, like Lehman Corporation, Atlas Corporation, and Tri-Continental Corporation, are listed on the New York Stock Exchange. Their stock can be purchased through a member broker at standard Stock Exchange commission rates, anything from one share to hundreds of shares. Prices of these stocks go up and down just as all other stocks do. Their worth depends on what the buyer is willing to pay and what the seller will accept in the light of the trust's earnings and the trend of the market. Sometimes an investment trust stock will sell at a premium price which is greater than its net asset value per share, and sometimes it will sell at a discount or below that value figure.

In contrast, shares of an open-end trust are always bought and sold on the basis of their net asset value, a figure that changes constantly because the value of the trust's investments quite naturally is always changing. Consequently, mutual funds compute and announce the net asset value for their shares twice daily, and this determines the price dealers will pay or charge.

The two kinds of trusts do much the same kind of business, but the difference in their setup makes for a difference in their operation. A closed-end trust cannot at will increase its original capital; an open-end trust not only can but usually wants to. And that's one reason why such strong merchandising effort is being put behind the open-end trusts today.

It's probably fair to say that most shares in a mutual fund aren't bought; they're sold — and sold by some pretty high-pressure, high-cost methods. To cover these selling costs, the buyer of a mutual fund is typically required to pay a commission or *loading charge* equal to 8% of the purchase price. If he wants to cash in his shares, he can usually do so without paying another commission, though sometimes a small redemption fee is charged. In contrast to that 8% figure, the buyer of a closed-end trust listed on any stock exchange would have to pay only a standard brokerage commission, typically 1% or 2% on purchase and another 1% or 2% on sale.

In addition to these charges, the owner of shares in an investment trust, whether it be open-end or closed-end, must also pay a management fee. In a typical case this fee comes to ½ of 1%, and the annual dividend which the trust pays is automatically reduced by the amount of the fee.

Of the 8% commission or loading charge, the dealer who sells the fund gets about 6%. Is it any wonder that mutual funds are so popular today with security dealers and most member firms of the New York Stock Exchange? On a $1000 order a broker makes $60. In contrast, on a $1000 order for a listed stock he makes a standard commission of only $15.

That's one reason why mutual funds grew from half a billion dollars to 3½ billions in the ten years from 1941 to 1951.

There are a number of people today who eye that phenomenal growth record with considerable misgivings. In some small part, this attitude can only be characterized as a hangover, traceable to the unsavory record that the investment trusts rolled up during the boom days of the twenties, a record that the trusts or *investment companies,* as they now prefer to be called, are strenuously trying to live down.

In those days, as the market roared to its 1929 high, investment trusts enjoyed an ill-starred boom. Open-end trusts were so new and insignificant then that they cannot be blamed at all, but the whole trust idea got a black eye. Almost every week, some new trust was born, and the little man clamored for a chance to buy its shares. Paeans of publicity made him believe this was his one big chance for a bandwagon ride to the promised land of perpetual prosperity.

But many of the trusts abused his confidence. They played fast and loose with his money. Trust-fund managers paid themselves large fees and bonuses for their somewhat questionable services. They split commissions with accountants and legal counsel to line their own pockets. Enjoying almost complete freedom to invest trust funds as they saw fit, the managers placed themselves too willingly at the service of investment bankers anxious to market new and dubious stock issues. They resorted to all kinds of speculative practices. They bought on margin. They pyramided paper profits. And they used the trusts to obtain control of whole industrial empires, often with only a paltry outlay of actual cash.

When the crash came in 1929, there were almost 700 investment trusts and they boasted "assets" of seven billion dollars, assets that were scattered like a handful of dry leaves when the big wind came. One big trust which had reported assets of over $150,000,000 was so hard hit that it publicly stated in 1932 that there was no point in trying to appraise the value of what was left from the wreckage, because it knew that the cost of making an inventory of its assets would actually exceed those assets.

The Securities & Exchange Commission, which has expressed concern about the growth of the funds, knows as well as anyone else that that particular chapter of history can't repeat itself, thanks to the *Investment Companies Act of 1940*. Under this law, no trust, closed- or open-end, can sell new shares in interstate commerce unless they are registered with the S.E.C. This means that a trust must make full and public disclosure of its investment policy and its financial situation. It means that no trust would buy on margin or sell short, even if it were sometime tempted to. It means, in effect, that the S.E.C. must be satisfied that the officers and directors of every trust are men of sound business experience and good moral character. And above all things, it means that the trusts can no longer be used as channels through which the investment banker can market questionable securities.

But the S.E.C. isn't so worried about the trusts slipping something over on it as it is about something much more fundamental: How stable would they prove to be in another period of economic stress? Would the big bubble burst again? This is a legitimate worry because in the structure of most mutual funds there is one contradiction that can spell trouble.

As a general rule, the mutual funds are particularly popular at a time when the market is going up. That's when the shares can be sold most easily. And yet that is precisely the time when it is most difficult and most risky for the fund to invest the new capital that comes flowing in.

Even more dangerous is the situation that might exist if

the market went into a tailspin. That's the time when people who owned shares in a mutual fund would be most tempted to cash them in, for that is when they as individuals would be most likely to need their savings. And yet that is precisely the time when it would be most difficult for a mutual fund to redeem its shares because to raise cash it would probably have to sell stocks from its portfolio.

Most funds of course have a cash reserve because even in a good year redemptions will run as high as 30% or 40% of the value of all new shares sold. But if there were a heavy run on the trust, it would have to sell off sizable blocks of stock to raise cash and it might very well have to take a loss on those forced sales. Additionally, those very sales might further depress the market and make it even more awkward for the trust to meet the next round of redemptions.

It's not always easy for a trust to buy good stocks at good prices in a rising market, but it would be much harder for it to sell 5000 shares of this or 10,000 shares of that at anything like a fair price in a declining market.

A good many economists share the S.E.C.'s concern about this situation. So do a few big brokerage firms that have refused to sell mutual funds. It is true that the trusts did well in meeting a challenge like this in 1946 when the market broke, but they were not then nearly so big as they are today, and the slump in stock prices was neither so severe nor so protracted as it might be some day.

The S.E.C. finds itself in an especially embarrassing predicament, because the mutual funds owe their great growth principally to the fact that they are regulated by the S.E.C.

It was the enactment of the 1940 law that reinspired public confidence in the trusts and touched off their meteoric rise.

The S.E.C. cannot restrain their growth, but it has thus far refused to relax some of the restrictions which the trusts feel are unnecessary. For example, the mutual funds cannot resort to any effective kind of printed advertising to stimulate sales. This is so because the funds are constantly issuing new stock, and under the Securities Act of 1933, no new securities issue can be advertised until it has been on the market for one year; it must be sold only on a prospectus basis. The S.E.C. says these rules apply to the mutual funds, and as a consequence the only advertising a fund can use is a "card ad," stating its name.

On the other hand, as long as the name of no specific mutual fund is mentioned, the broker or dealer who sells such shares can advertise, but he can only promote the desirability of owning mutual funds in general.

In these ads as well as in their door-to-door selling, the dealers lay heavy stress on the one great merit that the mutual fund unquestionably does have for the small investor — the protection it affords him through its diversified holdings in many different companies, many different industries.

If a man can afford to buy only one stock, he obviously takes less risk in buying a mutual fund than he does in buying even a "blue chip" stock with a good record for price stability and dividend payments. The blue chip may go up or it may go down; whichever way it goes, the investor's whole fortune must necessarily ride with it. All his eggs are in one basket.

But when he buys a share in a mutual fund, he spreads those eggs over a number of baskets because, in effect, he buys an interest in all the varied stocks the trust owns.

Of course, he might be able to achieve the same objective and at a decidedly lower commission cost by putting his money into a closed-end investment trust or by buying stock in a good fire and casualty insurance company, which is not unlike an investment trust because it too must invest its capital in a wide variety of stocks and bonds.

Mutual-fund salesmen also make quite a sales point out of the professional management which the shareholder gets for his money when he buys a mutual fund. They contend that the counsel which the small investor may get free from a broker is no substitute for this management. When the competitive selling gets really tough, they will argue that a broker can't afford to give small investors much assistance because he doesn't make enough out of the low brokerage commissions to cover the cost of a really adequate investment service — unless, they darkly hint, he induces the customer to switch from one stock to another to build commissions.

Actually, the argument that the mutual funds profit handsomely from skilled management sounds better than it is. Thus, from 1941 through 1952, according to *Forbes* magazine, 41 of the biggest mutual funds showed an increase in the value of their holdings of 146.5%. In this calculation, *Forbes* gave the funds the benefit of every doubt. Here's how: If a fund has a good year and profits by selling some stocks, it is likely to return a portion of such profit to its shareholders as a capital distribution; in its calculations *Forbes* assumed that all such distributions were promptly reinvested in the funds, thus helping them to improve their 12-year showing.

Now, a gain of 146.5% isn't bad from 1941 to 1952, but during the same period, the 90 representative stocks in Standard & Poor's Index showed an average gain of 151.2%.

This means that if an investor had picked at random any one of the 90 stocks in the index, chances are he would have made out a little bit better than if he had picked at random any one of the 41 investment trusts.

Nor is that the whole story. The 90 stocks in Standard & Poor's Index paid dividends over the twelve years which represented an average return of almost 6%. In contrast, dividends from mutual funds averaged only about 4%.

You may well think that the mutual fund is the best answer to your own investment problem. If you do, you should at least be careful to shop around before you buy. Don't say yes to the first salesman who knocks on your door. There are nearly 300 open-end investment trusts whose shares you can buy. Any one dealer may represent a few of these. Some obviously have better records than others, and some are less expensive to buy than others. While the loading charge or commission on a purchase runs around 8% on most funds, you can buy some at 7%, some at 6%, and some even lower than that. Again, management fees range from 2/10 of 1% up to 1%.

Some are better suited for one kind of investor than another. Some have their money invested wholly in common stocks, some wholly in bonds, and some in both. In some funds, the assets are wholly invested in the securities of a single industry, thus reducing the protection that can be had from well-diversified holdings.

Still other funds are risky because they operate in part on borrowed money — maybe as much as 30% of their total assets. Why should a fund borrow money? Because it thinks it can earn more on the securities it buys with the borrowed money than it will have to pay in interest on the loan. Such a fund is known as a *leverage fund,* and while its shares will go up more rapidly than those of other trusts when the market is rising, they will also go down more rapidly when the market falls. Some closed-end funds are also of the leverage type.

Finally, in shopping for a mutual fund, the investor should not be misled by mere size. While he probably ought not to put his money into a fund which has less than at least one or two million dollars in assets, the simple fact that another may have 400 million does not necessarily make it better for his purposes.

Where can the average investor get facts and figures to compare the various investment trusts if he wants to buy one? Some he can find in *Investment Companies,* an annual publication priced at $20 which is published by Arthur Wiesenberger & Company, 61 Broadway, New York 6, a brokerage firm that has long played a leading role in promoting investment trusts, particularly mutual funds. The same company issues a semi-monthly bulletin, *Investment Reports,* at $25 a year which consists principally of statistics and comment on closed-end trusts.

Investment Trusts and Funds — From the Investors' Point of View, published by the American Institute for Economic

Research, Great Barrington, Massachusetts, at a price of $1, may prove especially valuable because it undertakes to rate most of the leading trusts, both open-end and closed-end, and sets forth some of the pros and cons about all of them.

Another service dealing with investment trusts is, paradoxically, of greatest interest to the man who has decided to do his own investing rather than commit his funds to one of the trusts. The service, sold at $20 a year by Aigeltinger & Company, 52 Wall Street, New York 5, lists all the stocks owned by 14 big trusts and shows just exactly what proportion of their aggregate funds is invested in each. Published quarterly, the service thus shows which stocks are favored by the men responsible for the investment of more than a billion dollars and how their opinions of those stocks change from time to time.

Chapter 28
Why You Should Invest — If You Can

WHY should a man who has extra money invest it in stocks?
Here is the answer to that in one chart and one table.

The chart (see opposite page) shows the movement of stock prices from 1900 into 1952, as measured by Standard & Poor's long-term index of industrial stocks.

The table below shows the average annual *yield* on the stocks included in Standard & Poor's industrial index back to 1926, which is as far back as this series of statistics goes:

1926	4.86	1939	3.87
1927	4.73	1940	5.51
1928	3.93	1941	6.62
1929	3.61	1942	7.04
1930	4.84	1943	4.76
1931	6.40	1944	4.69
1932	7.74	1945	4.13
1933	4.06	1946	3.81
1934	3.37	1947	4.90
1935	3.52	1948	5.47
1936	3.39	1949	6.63
1937	4.83	1950	6.69
1938	4.96	1951	6.17

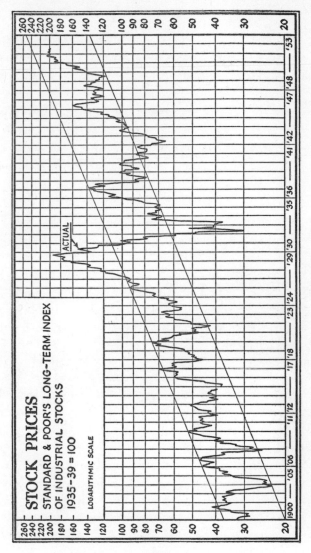

STOCK PRICES
STANDARD & POOR'S LONG-TERM INDEX
OF INDUSTRIAL STOCKS
1935-39 = 100

LOGARITHMIC SCALE

ACTUAL

1900 '05 '06 '11 '12 '17 '18 '23 '24 '29 '30 '35 '36 '41 '42 '47 '48 '53

CHART I

209

The yield figures shown in this table are arrived at by dividing the aggregate annual dividends paid on the various stocks by the aggregate value of the stocks at each year's end.

If the average price increases from one year to the next, the average dividend must increase proportionately or the yield will show a drop. But in the postwar years, yields steadily increased from about 4% to over 6% in 1950. This could have been the result of a decrease in the price of stocks or an increase in dividends.

Obviously, in this case it could only have been the result of a significant increase in dividends. Not only did stock prices *not* drop in this period, but they showed a whopping increase. On the chart, as you can see, the average price moved up from about 125 to better than 200 — a gain of 60%.

To illustrate what these figures really mean, suppose you had bought a stock at the representative price of $125 in 1946 and got a typical yield of 4%. That means your dividend would have been about $5. But in 1950, as the chart and table show, that same stock yielded over 6% on a price of $200, which would mean that it was paying an actual cash dividend of more than $12. Remember, however, you bought the stock at $125 and, computed on that purchase price, a $12 dividend in 1952 would represent an actual yield to you in that year of almost 10%.

The yield that an investor realizes from a stock is not affected in any way by changes in its price after he buys it; it is affected only by a change in the dividend. Thus, if you pay $100 for a stock paying $5, you realize 5% on your money, regardless of whether the stock drops to $80 or goes up to $120, as long as the $5 dividend is paid. If the dividend is increased to $6, you make 6%, and if it is reduced to $4, you make 4% — regardless of what happens to the price of the stock.

Now let's take another look at the chart. It shows that stock prices have moved generally upward for the past fifty years in a pretty well-defined path, excepting for that big peak in 1929 and that precipitous drop to 1932.

But isn't that a pretty big exception?

No, it isn't. Because under the stringent rules and regulations set by the Federal government and the Stock Exchange it seems impossible that we shall have to suffer again the kind of a speculative orgy which was responsible for that boom and crash.

Why has the trend of stock prices been steadily upward and why over any period of years is it likely to continue?

Because American business has grown steadily over the last fifty years, and there is every reason to believe it will continue to grow — continue to develop new products, new industries, new markets, and continue to expand all along the line.

That's one good reason for investing extra dollars in stocks. And there's a second one.

Take a look at the chart again (see page 212). Something new has been added — a second line showing the fluctuations of "the constant dollar" over the same period of years. This line is, in effect, a measure of purchasing power, since it shows how much the dollar is worth in terms of the *cost of living,* as computed by the Bureau of Labor Statistics.

When the cost of living goes up and the country is in a period of *inflation,* stock prices tend to rise for one reason:

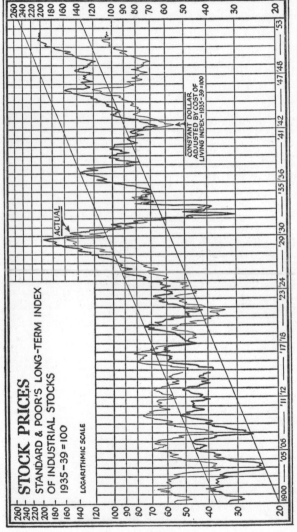

CHART II

"Constant dollar" is a measure of the purchasing power of invested dollars. It is arrived at by dividing the Standard & Poor average by the Bureau of Labor Statistics index for commodity prices. When the constant dollar is above 100 it means that invested dollars have more than kept pace with prices in terms of the 1935–1939 relationship; when it is below 100 the reverse is true.

212

Companies make and sell goods. When these goods are worth more in terms of dollars, the companies that make them are obviously also worth more in terms of dollars, and so are the shares of stock that represent the ownership of those companies. This is not true of all stocks, of course, but it is true of most stocks.

In periods of inflation, money that is invested in common stock or other property is not as likely to lose its purchasing power as money which is simply set aside in a savings bank or invested in bonds that have a relatively fixed value. Common stocks may not provide perfect protection against inflation but they will do until a better one comes along.

Certainly for the average man they are a better inflation hedge than real estate, for instance. Real estate prices usually rise too in a period of inflation, but it is not as easy for a man to be a good judge of real estate as it is to be a good judge of stock values; the element of risk is much greater. Furthermore, it is never so easy to dispose of real estate, particularly in a period of depression, if you suddenly need to raise cash. Finally, with real estate you have to contend with a great many other problems like taxes, repairs, and special assessments, whether or not it produces any income for you.

For all these reasons — for income, for a chance to see your capital grow, for the protection of its purchasing power — you may decide you want to invest in stocks.

But wait a minute. Maybe you shouldn't. Are you sure that those dollars you plan to put into the stock market are really extra dollars? Remember, there is an inescapable factor of risk in owning stocks, even the best of them. The averages may go up, but your stocks may go down. That is a risk worth taking for the man who isn't going to be seriously hurt in case he loses some of those dollars. But it's not a risk that a man should take if he's likely to need those dollars to meet some emergency.

What if there were a serious and expensive illness in the family? Are your savings adequate to meet that situation? What about the other expenses you may have to meet, such as the cost of a college education for your children? What about insurance? Have you got enough so that you are sure your family would be able to maintain at least a decent living standard if you were to die?

If you can answer yes to all these questions, you can and you probably should consider putting your extra dollars into common stocks.

Chapter 29
How You Should Invest — If You Can

THE stock you'd like to buy, of course, is the one that just doesn't exist. You'd like a stock that is completely safe, one that pays a liberal dividend, and one that's bound to go up.

There are a lot of good stocks that will probably satisfy you on any one of these counts, but none that will accomplish all three objectives.

If you want safety in a stock, you'll have to give up the hope that it will increase sensationally in value.

If you'd like to see your money grow, you have to be prepared to take a considerably greater measure of risk.

Sometimes it's possible to find either a fairly safe stock or one that seems likely to appreciate in price that will also yield you a better-than-average dividend. But even here, as a general rule, you can't have your cake and eat it too. If you get a liberal dividend, it's probably at the expense of one of the other two factors.

Hence, the first step in solving your investment problem is to decide on the one objective you most want to attain by your investments. Is it safety of capital? Or liberal dividends? Or price appreciation?

When you start thinking about stocks that might best match any of these objectives, you should first take a look at various industries and their future prospects. Remember the carriage industry was a thriving business thirty or forty years ago.

To see how these various factors might influence your own investment selections, consider how seven different people in widely varying circumstances might approach their investment problem.

Mr. Adams is twenty-six years old, unmarried, and as far as he can see likely to pursue his course of single blessedness for some time to come. Having received his college degree and completed his tour of duty in the army, he now has an excellent job as a chemist with a large food-manufacturing company. His income is $6000 a year, and thanks to the fact that he still lives at home, he can save at the rate of $1500 a year. With a $10,000 ordinary life insurance policy and a $5000 group policy issued by his company, he has made a start toward building an estate for himself.

With the savings which he accumulated while he was in the army, he now has about $3500, very little of which has to be earmarked for emergencies as long as his responsibilities are as light as they are. Then too, if he really got in a serious jam, he knows he could count on his folks to help him out.

He wants to see his capital grow, and so he wants to invest in stocks that have good growth possibilities, even though such stocks may yield only a scant return in dividends now.

Such a young man can afford to take a considerable measure of risk, but before he starts eying some of the more speculative stocks, he probably ought to put out an anchor to windward. Marriage has a way of creeping up on a man when he least expects it.

He can probably afford to invest $3000, and of this at least $1000 ought to go into the Series E government savings bond. Another $1000 might be divided between two solid common stocks — stocks that might be described as defensive in character because they have weathered many an economic storm in the past with little loss in value and with an unbroken record of dividend payments.

One of these might be a public utility like Pacific Gas & Electric or Consolidated Edison of New York. And the other one might be a stock like General Electric. Such a stock may fluctuate a little bit more as business expands or retracts, but it is still essentially stable because the company makes so many different products for so many different markets.

Mr. Adams might then very properly put his remaining $1000 into stocks of a more speculative nature — stocks with good growth possibilities. Maybe an aircraft stock. Maybe something in electronics. But probably first of all, a chemical stock — a field in which he should know firsthand something about new and promising developments.

As for his future savings — that $1500 he expects to accumulate each year — they too can go largely into growth stocks as long as his present situation remains unchanged. But he probably ought to start a systematic savings plan with his broker or he won't have those funds for investment.

Once he opens his brokerage account, Mr. Adams ought to figure on putting $125 a month into it and buying additional stocks as his funds grow. Most brokers will accept such cash deposits for future investment in a customer's account — some even pay a small amount of interest on them when they are finally invested — but brokers cannot go out and solicit deposits. If they advertised for them, they would be putting themselves into the banking business, at least in the eyes of state and federal banking commissioners, and the law says that no firm can be both a banker and a broker.

Consider now the case of Miss Baxter, a capable young lady of thirty-six. As an executive secretary in a large company, where she has worked for fifteen years, she now makes $110 a week, about as much as Mr. Adams. But age and sex can make a difference. She lives alone in a kitchenette apartment, responsible only to herself. She has no family to worry about, and she doesn't expect her mother and father, who live in a little town out West, ever to have to worry about her. She stands on her own feet.

A thrifty girl, she has managed over the years to put a little away every month. Now and again she has supplemented these savings with a special bonus check. Currently, she finds she is able to bank about $100 a month out of her salary. All told, she too has about $3500, a large part of it in E bonds, which yield just 2.9% and that only if they are held for the full ten years of their life.

Now Miss Baxter has decided she wants to invest in stocks. Why? Because every time she cashes a bond, the $100 she gets for it seems to buy less than it did the last time — less even than the $75 she paid for the bond ten years earlier. She wants to put her money into some investment where its purchasing power will be better protected and where she'll get a better return on her money. And if she's lucky, maybe she'll make a profit on her stocks — a big enough profit so that in five years she will be able to take that trip to Europe which she has always promised herself.

But maybe stocks will go down, her stocks included. That's a risk she has to take, and fortunately it's one she can afford to take. If stocks drop, she can probably wait for them to come back without any serious jeopardy, because her job offers her a good measure of security. Quite apart from her own medical and hospital insurance, she knows the firm will help her over any rough spots. And as for protection in her old age — well, the firm has an excellent pension program and that plus federal old-age insurance should take care of her quite handily.

What kind of stocks should Miss Baxter buy?

Obviously, she wants to be pretty conservative in her selections, but she probably doesn't have to make safety her sole objective. She can afford to take what's called a "businessman's risk," and she should look for stocks that pay liberal dividends.

Miss Baxter should put her money into a half-dozen different stocks — each of them a blue chip, each a leader in its own industry. Stocks like General Foods or Standard Brands, F. W. Woolworth or Safeway Stores, Standard Oil of New Jersey or Standard of California, General Electric or Westinghouse, American Tobacco or Liggett & Myers, plus one good utility.

She should put about $500 apiece into each of these half-dozen stocks. This means she will have to sell $3000 of her E bonds. She should sell the most recent ones and keep $500 worth of the oldest ones, because as those bonds get closer to their maturity dates, they pay a proportionately higher rate of interest.

When it comes to investing her future savings, a part of them might go into stocks representing still other industries and part of them into the best of the stocks she already owns.

Mr. and Mrs. Chandler face quite a different problem, despite the fact that Mr. Chandler's income as a skilled toolmaker in an auto-parts manufacturing plant is also about $6000 a year. To begin with, they live on a very modest scale in a small Ohio town. Still in their early thirties, they have been able to raise two children, now eight and ten, buy their own home, and still save a little bit.

They have only about $1000 in their bank account, but from now on that's going to grow fast. Mr. Chandler just made foreman last month, and that means $12.50 a week more in the pay envelope. Furthermore, in just a couple of months, the mortgage will be paid off, and they will have another $50 a month free and clear.

What it all adds up to is that they've got $1000 now, and they figure on having at least $1000 a year to invest from now on.

What about protection for his family? Mr. Chandler has a $5000 insurance policy, and he considers that plenty, in view of the benefit program which his union sponsors for all members.

He has become sold on stocks; he wants to go ahead right now, buying stocks in order to build a little estate.

That's a program that makes sense, provided he handles it right. He hasn't got a lot of money to put into the market, and to start with he wants to be sure that that money is well protected. What if one of his children had to be hospitalized for a long time with something like polio?

Where should he start? His local utility — the Ohio Edison Company — might be as good as any. The dividends will help pay his electric bill. That's an idea that has real appeal for Mr. and Mrs. Chandler.

After that, he might buy ten shares of a natural gas company, a stock that offers assurance of a fairly stable price, plus some possibilities of growth as natural gas consumption continues to grow.

His future investments for some time might be of much the same type — fairly stable stocks but ones that nevertheless offer some prospect of growth over the long pull. Nothing as spectacular as television or electronics, which market technicians might call "aggressive-growth situations," but perhaps something like the Canadian Pacific Railroad which stands to benefit over the years ahead as Canada pursues her certain course of expansion.

Mr. and Mrs. Davenport are a lot better off financially, but from an investment point of view they're really not as well off as the Chandlers. As one of the younger officers in a big advertising agency, Mr. Davenport makes $18,000 a year, but his scale of living is such that after taxes, mortgage payments on his $30,000 house, and premiums on a $50,000 life insurance policy, there's not much left over at the end of the year. Nothing more than he might need to pay an unexpected doctor's bill. His equity in the house — the unmortgaged part that he owns — and the cash value of his life insurance policy represent about all his savings.

But Mr. Davenport has struck it rich. He just got a special $5000 bonus, because he brought a new account into the agency last year. And Mr. Davenport knows exactly what he's going to do with that $5000. He's going to buy common stocks in two companies — two companies whose advertising his own agency handles. One of them is an aircraft manufacturer just ready to announce a new model light plane. Mr. Davenport is convinced that it is bound to become the first financial success in the field of private flying. The other company is a cigarette manufacturer with a new kind of filter, guaranteed to remove the nicotine.

Furthermore, the stocks of both these companies have high *leverage*. Mr. Davenport just learned about leverage, and what he knows about it makes both stocks look more promising in terms of quick profits.

A stock has high leverage if the company that issued it has a lot of bonds and preferred stock outstanding in relation to the amount of common stock. Here's how leverage works: Suppose the company has to pay half a million dollars in bond interest and preferred dividends every year. If it customarily makes only a million dollars' profit before the payment of such fixed charges, it has only a half million left for the common stockholders. But if the company suddenly makes three million dollars instead of one, it will have two and a half million dollars available for dividends on the common. In this situation, the company's profits would have tripled, but the amount of those profits available for dividends to the common stockholder or for reinvestment in the company would have been multiplied five times, since holders of the bonds and preferred stock would still get only their guaranteed half million.

With such an increase in profits, there might well be an extra dividend on the common stock, maybe even an increase in the annual rate of the dividend, and because of that prospect, the price of a high-leverage stock shoots rapidly ahead whenever its profit outlook is good. On the other hand, when the profit picture is bad, such a common stock drops more rapidly than do the more conservative stocks of companies that have no bonds or preferred stock outstanding.

When Mr. Davenport announces what he expects to do with his bonus, Mrs. Davenport puts her foot down. It sounds altogether too speculative for her. That money, she contends, should be set safely aside to assure a college education for their two children.

How should Mr. and Mrs. Davenport solve their problem? Probably two of those five thousand dollars ought to go into government bonds in case the family meets a real emergency. As for the balance, the stock of a good fire and casualty insurance company like Fidelity-Phoenix or Continental Insurance or American Insurance Company of Newark might represent a happy compromise between Mrs. Davenport's conservatism and Mr. Davenport's "all or nothing" impulse.

Since an insurance company must necessarily invest the

millions of dollars it collects from policyholders in something, and since a large proportion of those funds are invested in many different securities, the stock of such a company is apt to move as the general market average does — generally upward over the long term — but the swings in either direction, up or down, are not as pronounced because bonds make up a large part of an insurance company's holdings.

Ordinarily it would not be prudent for a man to put all his investment funds in a single security, but an insurance stock may be considered an exception because it does represent so many other securities.

Then too, Mr. Davenport is still only in his early forties and looks like a comer — the kind of man who will get a number of bonuses and salary increases. As time goes by, he will probably be buying other stocks, and to save on commission costs, he might just as well begin buying in good-sized units.

Mr. Edwards is a Nebraska wheat farmer. For fifteen years, life has been good to him. He has had good crops and got good prices for them. He is completely clear of debt on his farm and on his equipment, and all of it is in excellent condition. Insurance is no worry to him, because his boys, both of them in college now, could take over the farm and make a good living out of it if anything should happen to him.

He has $14,000 in extra capital, but he's beginning to wonder if he's doing the best be can with it. His oldest son started him thinking about that the last time he was home from college. Mr. Edwards has $4000 in savings bonds, $4000 in a local building and loan association, $3000 in a savings account, and about $3000 in his checking account.

Obviously, he has far more cash than he needs. One thousand dollars in his savings account and another thousand in his checking account should suffice, especially since that $4000 worth of E bonds is really the equivalent of cash and stands as an adequate backlog in case he has bad luck with his crops this year or has to make unexpected repairs to buildings or equipment.

Hence, he could prudently put $4000 cash into securities, and he probably ought to sell his $4000 worth of building and loan shares and invest that money in stocks too — a total of $8000. The building and loan shares yield him only 3½%, and he can get more for his money than that. Furthermore, they really represent an investment in real estate, and since his principal asset, the farm, is also real estate, it would seem wise for him to diversify his investments.

Here is a man who can really afford to take a fair measure of risk with his money for the sake of earning a better-than-average return, because he already has a substantial measure of protection — far more than most people have. In fact, he can afford to be a bit speculative in his selections.

First, it would be natural for him to invest in a good farm machinery stock — something like International Harvester — but he oughtn't to put too large a share of his $8000 into such a stock because if farmers suffer a reverse in their fortunes, so usually do the machinery manufacturers.

He might also properly invest in a company like Pillsbury or General Mills that processes the grain he raises.

But he might be better advised to put his money in the stocks of companies that have no relationship to his own business of farming — perhaps mining stocks like Anaconda Copper or Freeport Sulphur, or the automobile companies like General Motors or Chrysler, or chemical stocks like Du Pont, Monsanto, Dow, or Allied Chemical. Other stocks that might suit his situation would be Minnesota Mining & Manufacturing or Celanese or Carrier, because all of these companies operate in fields that show great future promise.

Mr. and Mrs. Frank are a retired couple, both over sixty-five. Old-age insurance plus small benefits accruing from a company pension plan are sufficient to provide an income of about $120 a month. Their only other assets consist of a home which they own free and clear and $35,000 in savings, most of it realized on annuities and life insurance policies in which Mr. Frank thriftily invested through the years.

On the other hand, if their assets are limited, so are their liabilities. Their two children are both married, and their futures are as secure as those of any people with moderate incomes can be.

The first impulse of Mr. and Mrs. Frank is to conserve what they have — to invest it in government or corporate bonds. But even with a 3% return ($1050 a year), their income from all sources would still be only about $48 a week.

Maybe they should put their $35,000 into high-grade common stocks that might pay them a 4% or 4½% dividend. That would mean an income of $1500 a year or so which, added to their basic $1440, would give them almost $57 a week.

226

But maybe Mr. and Mrs. Frank are placing too high a premium on safety by confining their selections to conservative stocks that will yield only 4% or 4½%. Just how happily could they live in their declining years on $57 a week? They could get by of course, but there certainly wouldn't be much left for any little luxuries. Nothing for an occasional trip to see the children and the grandchildren. And all their lives they'd looked forward to a little traveling after they had retired.

In a situation like that, might it not be better for them to take somewhat more risk with their money for the sake of more liberal dividends and perhaps an occasional profit on some stock? Maybe they could put as much as two thirds or three quarters of their money into the so-called "cyclical" stocks — stocks that follow the business cycle more closely. It would seem feasible for them to put $3000 into a good company in each of a half-dozen different fields — petroleum, mining, natural gas, automobiles, chemicals, maybe even steel or aircraft.

During a business decline, dividends might be reduced, and that could make things a little hard for them. But what if they did have to sell $500 or $1000 worth of stock in a bad year in order to make ends meet? At their age, they can afford to dip into capital if they have to without putting their lives in peril. And consider the rewards they might reap in a good year. Dividends of 8%, 10%, even 12% were not remarkable on cyclical stocks like General Motors and Kennecott Copper in the period of 1948 to 1952. And price increases of 20%, 30%, and 50% were commonplace.

227

For rewards like these, Mr. and Mrs. Frank can afford a sizable measure of risk on the bulk of their capital.

Finally, consider the situation of Mrs. Gordon, the fifty-seven-year-old widow of a successful doctor. Her principal assets consist of the family home and $95,000 worth of life insurance. True, the doctor did leave an assortment of stocks, but they proved to have a cash value of only about $5000, because, like most medical men who have little contact with business and less time in which to study it, Dr. Gordon had bought only the most speculative of securities — Canadian oil shares, stock in a plastic airplane company, and some preferred stocks that must have looked attractive because of big accumulations of back dividends — dividends that were owed but unfortunately never paid.

Mrs. Gordon doesn't want to see her capital dissipated that way. She wants to live off the income but leave the principal intact so that she can pass it along to her three children, all of them now well launched on substantial careers of their own.

Mrs. Gordon begins her calculations where every investor in such a situation must: "How much income do I have to have?" She figures she can manage comfortably on $4500 a year, which means, of course, that she must get a return of 4.5% on her $100,000.

Here is how her investment program might shape up:

(1) She should put $25,000 into Series K government bonds, yielding 2.76% interest.

(2) Another $25,000 should go into high-grade corporate

bonds and preferred stocks selected to provide a return of
3½% or better.

(3) With one half of her capital returning only about one
third of the income she needs, Mrs. Gordon must now look to
common stocks for the other two thirds of her income. She
must look for good stocks that will return an average of 6%
on her $50,000. Some of them will almost certainly be utilities,
because the stability of their operations makes for stability,
both of income and value. Some may be bank stocks selected
for similar reasons. But most of them will probably be industrials of the blue-chip variety — stocks that have paid good
dividends consistently for a long period of years.

More than a quarter of those listed on the New York Stock
Exchange can boast of such records running back at least
twenty years, and a third of these could also be classified as
the "bluest of the blue" because they are also the stocks of
companies that have no bonds outstanding, and little or no
preferred. Hence, all earnings or virtually all earnings are
available for dividends on the common; and this can be important in a period of bad business. These low-leverage stocks
— stocks like Coca-Cola, Du Pont, Eastman Kodak, General
Electric, Wrigley — are especially attractive to any conservative investor.

As a general rule Mrs. Gordon should not put more than
10% of the capital that she has for common-stock investments
into any one industry nor more than 5% into any one company. Furthermore, in judging the value of any particular
investment she might well make use of that old rule of
thumb, *"ten times earnings."* This means that a stock may

be considered reasonably priced if it sells at a figure roughly equal to ten times its earnings per share.

No one of the programs outlined for these seven investors is likely to fit your own situation. But a consideration of their problems and the way in which they might have been solved can serve to illustrate the kind of sober thinking that every investor must go through before he can hope to decide what stocks or bonds are right for him. Remember, there is no all-purpose security — no stock that fits ideally into every man's portfolio. Each man must work out his own investment salvation for himself.

That's why the best advice that was ever given is "Investigate before you invest." And the investigation should properly begin with your own financial situation.

Chapter 30
The Folklore of the Market

THE cheapest commodity in the world is investment advice from people not equipped to give it.

Many a man who doesn't own a share of stock still fancies himself as something of an authority on the market, and he's ready and willing to deliver himself of an opinion about it on the slightest provocation. As a matter of fact, if he actually owns stock himself, chances are you won't have to ask his opinion. He'll tell you what to buy, what to sell, and what's going to happen to the market. And you can't stop him.

The more a man knows about the market, the less he is willing to commit himself about it. The wisest of them all, old J. P. Morgan, when asked his opinion of the market, always used to reply, "It will fluctuate." He wasn't just being canny. He knew that was the only provable statement that could be made about the market.

Nevertheless, over the years, a number of generalizations about the market and about investing have come to be accepted as gospel. Actually, these homespun axioms must be accepted as little more than folklore. And like most folklore, each of them has a certain element of truth about it — and a certain element of non-truth.

For instance:

"Buy 'em and put 'em away."

This would have been a fine piece of advice if you had happened to buy $1000 worth of General Motors stock in 1921. By 1952, that stock would have been worth more than $15,000 and you would have collected over $13,000 in dividends.

But in 1921 the car everybody was talking about was the Stutz Bearcat, and there was a great deal of speculative market interest in Stutz stock. You might very well have decided to buy $1000 worth of that. How would you have made out on that purchase? The answer is that you would have lost all your money, and furthermore you would never have collected a penny in dividends.

The Stutz story is especially spectacular, but your experience with many another car might not have been too different. In 1939 the Temporary National Economic Committee listed the names of 812 different cars that had been produced in this country. Only 21 were then still alive. Some of those defunct cars lost out when their manufacturers were merged into General Motors or one of the other big auto companies, and the people who owned stock in those cars presumably got something for their money. But most cars vanished from the scene because their manufacturers went bankrupt.

Of course there is a measure of sense in the axiom. If you get to worrying about fluctuations of a point or two and try to buy and sell on every turn, you can pay out a lot of money in commissions needlessly and maybe end up with less profit than if you'd "bought 'em and put 'em away."

Nevertheless, it's also only good sense to remember that

securities are perishable. Values do change with the passage of time. Industries die, and new ones are born. Companies rise and fall. The wise investor will take a good look at all his securities at least once a year, and he could do worse than to ask his broker to review them with him then.

"You never lose taking a profit."

But you can.

Suppose you had put $50 into Sears, Roebuck in 1906. By 1940, the stock that you had bought would have been worth $1276 at its high. That would have been a nice profit — and you might have decided to take it.

But look what you would have lost. By 1952, that same stock was worth over $3400.

Of course, a profit *is* always a nice thing to have — in the pocket, not just on paper.

"If you wouldn't buy, sell."

A lot of people fall in love with their stocks and never think about selling them. A few years ago a New York Stock Exchange survey showed that a third of the people who owned stock had never sold any. They had just bought, presumably leaving the stock to be sold by their estates someday.

Unquestionably many of these stock owners could and should have sold some of their holdings somewhere along the line, investing the proceeds in stocks that would have been better suited both to the times and their own changing situation.

You can get a surprisingly objective look at the stocks you own by asking yourself periodically if you would buy them again at their prevailing prices, assuming you had the money.

If the answer is no on some of them, you may at least want to consider the advisability of selling them.

Of course, the answer may not be either a flat yes or no, for there are times when you can be pretty neutral about a stock, even one you own, times when it pays to "wait and see."

"Buy when others are selling. Sell when they buy."

This sounds like a neat trick if you can do it.

Obviously, you can't make money if you consistently buck the trend of the market. Where, for instance, would you have been if you had been selling stocks all through the postwar bull market?

So the trick lies in anticipating the action of all the others — in buying just before the crowd decides to buy and selling just before they do. This is just exactly the trick that the exponents of various formula plans try to turn by hitching their buying and selling operations to some arbitrary decline or advance in the market.

Others, less scientific, simply try to sell at the tops and buy at the bottoms. But how do you know when the market hits bottom? How far down is down?

Make no mistake about it: Anyone who tries to practice this fine art is "playing the market" in the purest sense of the word. He's speculating; he's not investing.

"Don't sell on strike news."

There's some truth to the old adage. Nowadays labor troubles in any big company or in an industry are apt to be pretty well publicized. Consequently, the market is likely to have discounted the possibility of a strike during the time it was brewing; the stock will already have gone down in price, and it may even advance when the strike news breaks.

Again, many people think that a strike doesn't really damage a company's long-term profit picture. They contend that while a strike is on, demand for the company's products is only deferred, and as soon as the strike is over, it will enjoy better business than ever.

But such a theory is often little more than wishful thinking. After all, most strikes end with the company facing a higher labor bill. And many times the demand for its products which a company couldn't fill while its employees were on strike has been happily filled by a competitor.

"Don't overstay the market."

A fine piece of advice, but how do you know when to sell and take your profit — if that's what you're interested in?

Sometimes you can tell by watching those basic business indicators that show what's happening to production, distribution, and consumption of goods. But sometimes you can't because the market, especially since World War II, doesn't seem to be paying too close attention to them.

Nevertheless, if business appears to be on the skids, and the stock market is still boiling merrily upward, sooner or later there's going to be a reckoning.

"Always cut your losses quickly."

Nobody wants to ride all the way downhill with a stock if the company is headed for bankruptcy, but at the same time you don't want to be stampeded into a sale by a price decline that may have no relationship to the fundamental value of the stock.

Remember, the price of a stock at any time reflects the supply and demand for that stock, the opinions and attitudes of all the buyers and all the sellers. If a stock is closely held, if its *"floating supply"* — the amount usually available in the market — is limited, the price of that stock can be unduly depressed for quite a period if some large holder is selling a sizable block of it, just because he may need the cash and not because he thinks the less of it.

"An investor is just a disappointed speculator."

This cynical observation has a measure of truth in it. Every stock buyer hopes for a big, fat profit, even if he won't admit it to himself. So when the market drops, he does the best he can to assuage his disappointment by assuring himself and everybody else that of course he never expected to make a killing . . . he was just investing on the basis of the fundamental stock values.

This is especially true of that congenital bull — the odd-lot buyer. As a class, the odd-lotters always buy more than they sell. And sadly, they are apt to buy only when the market is already too high.

So often does this happen that some speculators gauge their own actions by the volume of odd-lot purchases. When that volume expands, they sell.

But in the long run, the small investor often has the last laugh. After all, the stock market has gone pretty steadily up for fifty years, hasn't it? And since the odd-lot man is a heavy buyer of the market leaders — the 100 stocks that usually account for two thirds of the Exchange volume — he has made out pretty well over the long pull.

On the other hand, many a big speculator like Daniel Drew has died broke.

"*A bull can make money. A bear can make money. But a hog never can.*"

That's one to remember.

The desire to make money leads most people into the market. Call it ambition or greed, it remains the prime motivating force of our whole business system, including the stock market.

But greed is always dangerous. It's an engine without a governor.

So you made a killing once in the market. Good. You were lucky. Don't think you can make one every day.

If you own a good stock, one that's paying you a good return on your money and seems likely to go on doing so, hang onto it. Don't keep switching your stocks, looking for greener pastures. And forget about the other fellow and the killing he made — or says he made. Maybe he can afford to speculate.

But if you're an investor, act like one.

Chapter 31
Who Owns Stock?

IF Wall Street didn't exist, it would be necessary to invent it. In fact, that's just exactly what our forefathers did.

Why must there be a Wall Street?

Because, in our economy, capital like labor must be free to work where it wants to. If you've got extra dollars, you've got the right in our society to say where you want to put them to work in order to make more dollars.

And that's a right which would be a pretty empty one if there weren't some means for you to transfer your funds from one enterprise to another when you wanted to.

Wall Street provides that means. It's a market place for money.

And in the past twenty years, it has played an increasingly important role in our economy. It has made it possible for millions of people to put their savings to work in American business. That has been good for them, good for business, and good for the whole country.

Time was when only the wealthy people owned stocks and bonds. That's not true any longer. For one thing, there aren't so many wealthy people as there used to be. The millionaire is the vanishing American.

If business is to have the money it needs to go on growing,

somebody has got to take the rich man's place. That somebody can only be the investor of moderate means — thousands of such small investors, because it takes a thousand of them with $1000 each to equal the million dollars in capital that one wealthy man may have supplied yesteryear. And tomorrow it will take many, many more thousands of them, because the economic revolution in this country has not yet run its course.

Wall Street bears the primary responsibility for recruiting those new investors. Wall Street and all its counterparts throughout America — La Salle Street in Chicago, Montgomery Street in San Francisco, Marietta Street in Atlanta, and Main Street in many a Middletown.

Wall Street takes its responsibility seriously. Every year it puts millions of dollars into booklets, pamphlets, and letters to explain securities. It uses educational advertising — newspapers, magazines, television, radio, even carcards and billboards. It has taken the story of stocks and bonds to county fairs and women's clubs. It has even put the story into movies that any group can show free of charge.

How well has Wall Street done with all this educational effort in stimulating new investor interest?

Better than you might think — but not nearly as well as it must.

Not until June 1952 did Wall Street know just how it stood on the job. Strange as it may seem, nobody knew just how many stockholders there were in the country until the New York Stock Exchange got the Brookings Institution to find out. American Telephone & Telegraph knew it had 1,200,000 stockholders. And thirty other big companies knew they had more than 50,000 apiece. But nobody knew just what duplication there was in those stockholder lists. And nobody knew the grand total for all companies.

The Brookings Institution says that total is 6,490,000, representing a little more than 4% of all individuals and just about 10% of all the families in the country. Disappointing as that total figure was when it was announced, Wall Street found encouragement in the fact that about one fifth of the total had become stockholders in the preceding three years.

Here are other key figures from the report:

Men and women own stock in just about equal numbers.

More than half of all stocks are owned by people over fifty.

Over 40% of the people who went to college own stock.

Stock ownership is proportionately higher in the far-western states than anywhere else.

Most stockholders own shares in only one or two companies — 46% in one and 16% in two.

Two thirds of all stockholders have owned stock for eight years or more.

People with family incomes of less than $2000 account for 4.3% of all shareowners.

While a little over half the people who make more than $10,000 a year own stock, it's the $5000–$10,000 group which accounts for the greatest number of stockholders — 2,080,000 of them or 44% of the total.

Why don't more people invest — the people who can afford to?

There's one clear-cut answer to that. They don't understand

stocks and bonds, and what people don't understand they are apt to be afraid of.

We may be the richest nation in the world, the very bulwark of a modern and enlightened capitalism, but the blunt fact of the matter is that we as a nation are financially illiterate.

A year or two before the Brookings survey, the New York Stock Exchange undertook to find out just how much — or rather how little — America knew about securities. For this job it retained the Public Opinion Research Corporation.

In this survey people were asked just how they would invest money if they had some extra cash, and to make the problem as easy as possible the researchers suggested six possible channels of investment — government bonds, corporate bonds, stocks, life insurance, real estate, and savings banks. You could divide the money up any way you liked — all of it in one or a little in each.

Here are the kinds of investment and the proportion of the people who favored putting at least some money into each of them.

Government Bonds	83%
Life Insurance	67%
Savings Banks	43%
Real Estate	42%
Stocks	16%
Corporate Bonds	13%

To see just how much knowledge and understanding lay behind those selections, the researchers then told the people to assume that ten years of steadily rising prices lay ahead of them.

"Would they, in that situation," the researchers asked, "see any disadvantage to owning government bonds?"

More than half of the people — 56% of them — blandly said no. They could see no disadvantage to having their money in an investment with a fixed-dollar value in a period of inflation!

Yes, ignorance is unquestionably the biggest deterrent to investing. But there's another factor in the picture too. Successful investing isn't simple. It means thinking your own investment problem through to a logical conclusion. It means being willing to study the facts about various securities. It means checking up on a stock before you buy it and after you buy it.

That's not easy admittedly. But it's not beyond the capabilities of any of us. Not if Nicholas J. Harvalis could do it. Maybe you saw the story in the newspapers a couple of years ago about him — the uneducated immigrant who worked all his life in restaurants for a wage that never exceeded $125 a month but who managed to leave an estate of $160,000.

Here is how he did it as related by his counselor, Max D. Fromkin of Omaha:

Fromkin & Fromkin
Keeline Building
Omaha Nebraska 2

February 13th, 1951

I give you now the story of NICHOLAS J. HARVALIS, late of Omaha, Nebraska, who departed this life on the last day of the month and year of 1950, to wit, December 31, 1950, shortly after the close of the market for the year.

Nicholas was a friend of mine for over 25 years, and during that time I was his attorney and counselor.

Nicholas came to this country from Greece at the age of 15 years. He was without education and money, and he immediately went to work as a waiter in various cafés and restaurants operated by his countrymen in Omaha at wages which provided a bare living for him.

He was unmarried and lived the many years in Omaha alone in a modest room.

He was thrifty to the point of many times denying himself the comforts of life in order to save from his earnings sufficient to make investments for his security and old age. He employed his leisure hours reading and studying financial papers and books. He also spent many hours in the Public Library poring over history and philosophy.

On May 18, 1927, he became a citizen of the United States by naturalization. He was a firm and optimistic believer in the opportunities offered the common man in the United States, and he believed that the greatest return in investments was in common stocks of well-managed companies.

Thus, beginning about 1937, he started a systematic purchase of common stocks. His early investments were in National Distillers, Laclede Gas, General Motors, S. S. Kresge, Atlantic Refining, International Nickel, J. C. Penney, General Electric. He bought a few shares in each of these companies and added to them from time to time.

He kept meticulous records of all of his transactions, including dividends received. His dividends, which at first were modest, he would save and reinvest in these same stocks.

He subscribed to the Wall Street Journal and avidly read the paper from cover to cover. As a matter of fact, at the time of his death the only thing in his room apart from bare furnishings was a neat stack of issues of the Wall Street Journal for the last two years.

In 1943, he began selling stocks for long-term profits when he felt the market was high, and later he began a repurchasing program.

In 1943, his earnings from wages as a waiter and soda jerk in a local drug store known as the Paxton Pharmacy at 15th & Harney Streets in Omaha were $1,602.00, while his income from dividends of common stocks was $1,825.00.

In 1944, his earnings from wages were $1,525.000, and his dividends from common stocks rose to $2,285.00. In the same year he made from gains in the sale of stocks the sum of $2,600.00.

In 1945, his wages were the same, but dividends from stocks came to $2,785.60. Long-term profits in that year were $7,713.84.

In 1946, he began acquiring Cities Service stock.

In 1946, his dividends from stocks fell to $1,506.24, but his gains on the sale of stocks were very substantial.

In 1947, his dividends rose to $2,191.24.

In 1948, his dividends were $10,562.98.

In 1949, his dividends were $7,081.24.

In 1950, his dividends were $10,095.50.

During all these years he earned from wages as a soda jerk a sum not to exceed $1600 per year.

When he died on December 31, 1950, he was the owner of the following common stocks:

1370 shares Cities Service common
 200 shares Boeing common
 300 shares Rock Island common
 100 shares General Electric common
 200 shares American Bank Note common
  40 shares of Hearst Consolidated Publications 7% preferred
 200 shares of Great Northern Iron Ore.

The above shares had an approximate value at the time of his death of $160,000.00.

Nicholas J. Harvalis kept perfect records and had in his room every statement from his broker of every transaction he had ever made. In addition he made accurate reports for income tax purposes and was proud to pay his government every cent of tax for the privilege of his citizenship and the opportunity that his government gave him.

In my association with him as his attorney I found him always to be a very polite, mild-mannered, and courteous individual. He was often asked for advice on the market and was always very cautious to mention only highly rated dividend-paying stocks.

Nicholas amassed this huge sum, considering his limitations, and in his death he leaves to his brother and sisters (11 of them) in Greece a substantial inheritance, which they will no doubt spend more freely and with less good judgment than the man who earned it.

Very truly yours,
MAX FROMKIN

Few of us would be willing to pay the price Mr. Harvalis did for his achievement. But then most of us would be willing to settle for just a small measure of that success — the success that can be achieved not by luck, not by "inside tips," not by speculation, but by prudent and intelligent investing.

Index of Terms and Titles

The securities business uses many special terms and phrases, which have been italicized in the text where they are first used. These are listed here together with the names of companies, government agencies, publications, and people also dealt with in the book.

For some general terms (*common stock, investor, speculator*) only the first reference is listed because, as the chapter headings indicate, these are the words the whole book is about.

INDEX OF TERMS AND TITLES